Comments and reviews about the 1st Edition of Quick & Hea

"Here's one cookbook that lives up to its name..." —**Cooking Light Magazine**

"Many new cookbooks include the word 'healthy' in the title, but if you're looking for information and recipes that are also quick and useful, this cookbook will be a good investment." —**The Oregonian**

"Well organized, well-thought-out, takes into account how busy most of us really are...This could become a kitchen stand-by for busy cooks..." —**Miami Herald**

"A lifesaver for real-world cooks....with a wealth of dietary hints and shortcuts." —**BookPage**

"One way to eat healthier: modify fat-laden recipes. *Quick & Healthy* is one of ten that the National Center for Nutrition and Dietetics suggest you consider." —**USA Today**

"A great book to recommend to clients, family and friends." —**Kathryn Miller, MS, RD, LD, Staff Nutritionist, Cooper Clinic, Dallas, Texas**

"*Quick & Healthy* is just what everyone is looking for - wonderful sounding recipes that can be prepared in minutes. It's a book that dietitians will feel confident in recommending as well as giving for a gift." —**Marion J. Franz, RD, MS, CDE., Vice President, Nutrition and Publications International Diabetes Center, Minneapolis, Minnesota**

"The recipes are designated to be low in fat and cholesterol, yet high in taste. The nutritional analysis can help you assess how these simple meals can enhance your food plan. I recommend that you take the time to buy this book..." —**Nancy Clark, MS, RD, Sports Nutritionist and author of *Nancy Clark's Sports Nutrition Guidebook***

"At last. Practical tips for controlling fat and cholesterol, along with quick, healthy recipes that taste great. Highly recommended." **—John P. Foreyt, PhD, Director, Nutrition Research Clinic, Houston, Texas**

"Resolutions to eat healthier are easy to do using *Quick & Healthy*. The recipes work, and what's more, they taste like you've been slaving over them for hours." **—The Single Parent**

"Just what people are looking for—a user friendly book about a lower fat, higher complex carbohydrate eating style." **—Sonja L. Conner, MS,RD, Research Associate Professor, Oregon Health Sciences University and co-author of** *The New American Diet* **and** *The New American Diet System*

"*Quick & Healthy* is not just another cookbook. The Time Saving Ideas and Quick Meals and Snacks make the book more like a kitchen almanac... A must-have for today's busy cooks!" **—Peggy Paul, RD,LD, Director, Oregon Dairy Council**

"Her book offers great time saving tips, practical nutrition information and easy-to-prepare recipes. More than a traditional cookbook, *Quick & Healthy* is an anthology of ideas for healthy living." **—Focus on Books**

"This cookbook targets all of us who claim we do not have time to eat healthfully. It is an attractive, practical book with each recipe being on a single page... A worthwhile addition to any 'eat and run' kitchen." **—Lipid Clinic News**

"Easy-to-fix recipes for low-fat meals." **—The Columbian, Vancouver, WA**

"These quick-fix meals don't skimp on health." **—The Register-Guard, Eugene, OR**

"Brenda's a mom, too, and knows what it takes to try to make <u>all</u> the eaters in the family happy." **—Farmers Advance**

"*Quick & Healthy Recipes and Ideas* contains easy-to-follow, healthful recipes that your family will actually eat." **—California Health**

Quick &
healthy
Low-fat · Carb Conscious Cooking
SECOND EDITION

by Brenda J. Ponichtera
registered dietitian

COVER & DESIGN: Lisa Becharas
ILLUSTRATIONS: Janice Staver

SCALEDOWN PUBLISHING, inc.   The Dalles, Oregon

Library of Congress Control Number: 2004095957

Publisher's Cataloging-in-Publication

    Ponichtera, Brenda J.
      Quick & healthy low-fat, carb conscious cooking /
    Brenda J. Ponichtera. — 2nd ed.
      p. cm.
      Includes index.
      Rev. ed. of: Quick & healthy recipes and ideas.
      LCCN 2004095957
      ISBN 0-9629160-2-1

      1. Low-cholesterol diet—Recipes. 2. Low-fat diet—
    Recipes. 3. Diabetes—Diet therapy—Recipes.
    4. Low-carbohydrate diet—Recipes. 5. Quick and easy
    cookery.   I. Ponichtera, Brenda J. Quick & healthy
    recipes and ideas. II. Title. III. Title: Quick and
    healthy low-fat, carb conscious cooking.

    RM237.75.P65 2005   641.5'63
                  QBI04-200346

Cover & Design: Lisa Becharas
Illustrations: Janice Staver
Editing: Mary Schlick
Cover Photography: Marcus Swanson Photography, Inc.

Printed in the United States of America
10 9 8 7 6 5 4 3 2 1

Published by: ScaleDown Publishing, Inc.
1519 Hermits Way
The Dalles, Oregon 97058
Phone: 541-296-5859   Fax: 541-296-1875
e-mail: scaledwn@gorge.net   •   http://www.quickandhealthy.net

o the three special men in my life,

Ken, Kevin and Kyle
for your love and support

to my fellow Street Walkers,

Jana Webb, Yvonne Lorenz, Claudia Schon, Sandra Fritz,
Connie Christensen, Joyce Lehman and Charlotte Johnson

for your miles of support throughout this marathon called Life.

Acknowledgements

I could never do this alone. Thank you to the following for helping me to make this book a reality.

My husband, Ken - grocery shopper and recipe tester. Thanks for helping me survive another edition.

My sons, Kevin and Kyle for your support and willingness to sample whatever I cook.

My administrative assistant, Nancy Taphouse, for your dedication to this project and your commitment to helping me do it right. I couldn't do it without you.

Graphic designer, Lisa Becharas, who is one of the best. Her creativity is exceptional.

Illustrator, Janice Staver, a friend and very fine artist.

My editor Mary Schlick, for helping catch the little things.

The computer specialists who worked miracles: Scott Thompson and Larry Hales.

My printer, Bruno Amatter, who continues to hold my hand through the production process. Don't ever let go.

Recipe testers and recipe contributors, Claudia Schon, Nancy Taphouse, Carol Beer, Yvonne Lorenz, Jana and Rocky Webb, Ellie Timinski, Sandra Fritz, Connie Christensen, Charlotte Johnson, Joyce Lehman, Debbie Kelly, Mike Newman, Jane Lyon, and Anita Clason.

The many professionals who have helped me along the way: Elizabeth Somer, MA, RD, Tracy Dugick, MS, RD, CDE, Karmeen Kulkarni, MS, RD, CDE, Kathy Isoldi, MS, RD, CDE, Hope S. Warshaw, MMSc, RD, CDE, Nancy Clark, MS, RD, Madelyn L. Wheeler, MS, RD, CD, CDE, Anne Daly, MS, RD, CDE, Kathy McManus, MS, RD, Kelly Chambers, MS, RD, CDE, Karen Deuster, MS, RD, Connie Evers, MS, RD, Bridget Swinney, MS, RD.

And lastly, to all of the people who use my cookbooks and have offered kind words of praise and stories of success - you have been my inspiration!

Table of Contents

Recipe Notes

Sodium
Salt is listed as an optional ingredient in the recipes and is therefore not included in the nutrient analysis of the recipe. When possible, canned products without the addition of salt, or reduced-salt were used. These are noted with an asterisk (*) and the notation: *Sodium is figured for reduced-salt.*

Fiber
Fiber is listed in the nutrient analysis of each recipe. Recipes that provide significant fiber also include one of the following notations:
    for 3-4 grams of fiber - *One serving is a good source of fiber.*
    for 5 or more grams of fiber - *One serving is an excellent source of fiber.*

Carb Servings and Food Exchanges
When calculating Carb Servings and Food Exchanges, the fiber is subtracted from the total carbohydrate if one serving of a recipe has 5 or more grams of fiber. To indicate this, the headings "Carb Servings" and "Exchanges" are followed with an asterisk (*) and the following notation is at the bottom of the nutrient analysis: *reflects carbohydrate minus fiber*

Fat
A few recipes are higher in fat. However, the type of fat is heart-healthy. These recipes are followed with the notation: *Most of the fat in this recipe is heart-healthy monosaturated and /or polyunsaturated fat.*

Optional Ingredients
Ingredients listed as optional are not included in the nutrient analysis for each recipe. If a choice of ingredients is given, the first one is used in the nutrient analysis.

Nutrient Analysis
Figures have been rounded. If the value is less than .5, it is rounded down to zero. If the figure is .5 or more, it is rounded up to one. The following abbreviations are used: g = grams, mg = milligrams.

Introduction

Take something good and make it even better. With that in mind, I set out to totally revise my first book, *Quick & Healthy Recipes and Ideas*. The name is changed to more accurately reflect the content, which has also been changed to meet the concerns of today's consumers.

My focus is still health conscious people who don't want to spend a lot of time in the kitchen. This includes families who want to eat more healthfully, people with diabetes or heart disease and also those wanting to lose weight.

With over two hundred recipes, I have added over sixty new ones and revised many of the old favorites. My emphasis is on low-fat, low-cholesterol, high fiber, while still appealing to carb conscious individuals, whether their concern for carbohydrates is due to diabetes or weight loss.

I've tried to focus on the sensible use of carbs (carbohydrates) by using high fiber foods, when possible, and limiting simple carbohydrates. Artificial sweeteners are included as an alternate to sugars when workable in the recipes.

In developing the recipes and all of the practical information in this book, I have kept in mind the following three goals that can lead to healthier living:

Achieving and maintaining a desirable weight
Eating more high fiber carbohydrates and fewer simple carbohydrates
Eating a low-fat diet, while using monosaturated and polyunsaturated fats, limiting saturated fats and avoiding trans fats

Each recipe includes diabetes and weight loss exchanges, nutrient analysis and carb servings. The information not only helps those with dietary concerns but also provides information to the health conscious consumer.

This book is more than a cookbook. I have also included practical nutrition guidelines, weight loss tips, time saving ideas, recipes listed by carb servings, information on food products and menus. All are designed to help you eat better and save time.

I hope using this book will bring you and your family closer to good health.

Brenda J. Ponichtera
Registered Dietitian

Using Artificial Sweeteners

All brands of artificial sweeteners are not alike and you may prefer the taste of one over another. Some people note an undesirable aftertaste with some artificial sweeteners but this seems to be an individual preference.

To offer another option for reducing calories and carbohydrates, we used artificial sweeteners as an alternative to sugars in a number of recipes. Listed below is what you can expect when using an artificial sweetener.

Non Baked Recipes

Artificial sweeteners usually work well with foods that do not require baking. Cooking with artificial sweeteners is usually very acceptable if the recipe is not one that is expected to brown or rise.

Baked Recipes

Real sugar offers certain qualities to baked goods that artificial sweeteners do not. Real sugar helps baked goods to brown, contributes to the volume, adds moistness and tenderness, and helps the baked foods stay fresh longer.

You may note the following when artificial sweetener is used in place of all, or part, of the sugar:

> Cakes or muffins don't rise very well.
> The baked item does not brown.
> Baking time is often decreased.
> The flavor may need to be improved by adding vanilla extract.
> Baked goods will spoil more quickly if not stored in the refrigerator.

Some of the baked recipes in this book use artificial sweetener for part of the sugar. These recipes were considered acceptable by our recipe testing staff. However, the quality is not consistent with the same recipe made with all sugar and you may note some of the changes listed above. We did not use artificial sweeteners in recipes when the result was not acceptable.

Note: When using an artificial sweetener, refer to the label for the amount to substitute for sugar.

Food Exchanges for Diabetes and Weight Loss

Exchange lists are used in many weight loss programs and diabetic diets.

There are six food groups or exchange lists. In forming the exchange lists, foods with similar calories, carbohydrate, protein, and fat are grouped together.

By following a meal pattern based on the exchange lists, one can "exchange" a food in one group for another food in the same group. This method helps to increase variety while at the same time keeping calories and nutrient values fairly consistent.

The six exchange lists are: starch, fruit, milk, nonstarchy vegetables, meat and meat substitutes, and fat.

The meat and meat substitute list and the milk list are further divided into groups based on the amount of fat a food contains. The leanest meats and the nonfat/low-fat dairy products are the best choices.

Please be aware that the calories, carbohydrate, protein and fat used for each exchange list are averages and are not always the exact values for a specific food within the exchange list.

Recipes with less than 20 calories per serving are listed as "free" for one serving. If you eat more than one serving and the calories exceed 20, the food is not considered "free" and should be counted as an exchange.

When calculating exchanges for recipes with five grams of fiber or more, the fiber was subtracted from the total carbohydrate when figuring the exchanges. However, calories and total carbohydrate, listed in the nutrient analysis, are not changed.

Each recipe in this book has the exchanges listed. The figures used to calculate the exchanges are from the Exchange Lists for Meal Planning by the American Diabetes Association and American Dietetic Association. For more information on the exchange lists, contact a registered dietitian or your local American Diabetes Association.

Carb Servings

All recipes in this book include Carb Servings also known as Carb Choices. The general rule is 15 grams of carbohydrate equals 1 Carb Serving.

If a serving/portion of food has 5 grams of fiber or more, the grams of fiber are subtracted from the total carbohydrate when figuring Carb Servings. If the fiber is less than 5 grams, it is not subtracted from the total carbohydrate.

Refer to the section titled **Recipes Listed by Carb Servings** for more information and for a listing of recipes grouped by category and Carb Servings. This listing also includes calories, fat, carbohydrate, fiber and food exchanges for each recipe.

The following chart was used to convert carbohydrate to Carb Servings.

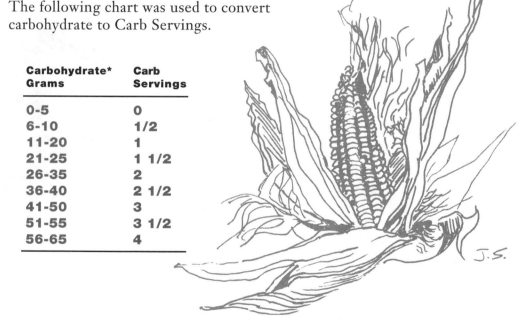

Carbohydrate* Grams	Carb Servings
0-5	0
6-10	1/2
11-20	1
21-25	1 1/2
26-35	2
36-40	2 1/2
41-50	3
51-55	3 1/2
56-65	4

*This value is the total carbohydate for one serving/portion minus the grams of fiber if the fiber is 5 grams or more for each serving/portion.

Recipes Listed by Carb Servings

Following is a ten page table, listing recipes that are grouped by Carb servings. The information below will help you when using the table:

The carbohydrate in one portion/serving of the recipe was used to figure Carb Servings. See page 12 for the conversion chart.

Food Exchanges are also listed for one portion/serving of the recipe.

Recipes with less than 20 calories per portion/serving are listed as "free" for one serving. If you eat more than one serving and the calories exceed 20, the food is not considered "free" and should be counted as an exchange.

Some recipes are listed twice if the nutrient analysis is provided for both artificial sweetener and regular sugar.

If the fiber is 5 grams or more for one portion/serving, the grams of fiber are subtracted from the total carbohydrate when figuring Carb Servings and Exchanges. However, the calories and total carbohydrate listed are not changed.

Below is the number of recipes listed by Carb Servings that are in the table that follows:

53 recipes with 0 Carb Servings	(0 – 5 grams of carbohydrate)
46 recipes with 1/2 Carb Serving	(6 – 10 grams of carbohydrate)
55 recipes with 1 Carb Serving	(11 – 20 grams of carbohydrate)
36 recipes with 1 1/2 Carb Servings	(21 – 25 grams of carbohydrate)
32 recipes with 2 Carb Servings	(26 – 35 grams of carbohydrate)
2 recipes with 2 1/2 Carb Servings	(36 – 40 grams of carbohydrate)
2 recipes with 3 Carb Servings	(41 – 50 grams of carbohydrate)

The following recipes are 0 Carb Servings for one portion.

0-5 grams of carbohydrates are counted as 0 Carb Servings.

	Calories	Total Fat Grams	Total Carb Grams	Dietary Fiber Grams	Food Exchanges
BEVERAGES					
Cran-Raspberry Cooler	15	0	4	0	Free
Wine Cooler	80	0	1	0	2 fat
APPETIZERS					
Beef Lettuce Wraps - 1 wrap	59	3	1	0	1 lean meat
Chicken Lettuce Wraps - 1 wrap	44	1	1	0	1 vl meat
Chinese Barbecued Pork	47	2	2	0	1 lean meat
Creamy Seafood Dip	32	1	1	0	1/2 lean meat
Hot Artichoke and Spinach Dip	70	4	4	2	1 vegetable, 1 fat
Mock Sour Cream	15	0	1	0	Free
Shrimp Lettuce Wraps - 1 wrap	43	0	1	0	1 vl meat
Shrimp Lettuce Wraps - 1 wrap**	40	0	1	0	1 vl meat
Smoked Salmon Spread	52	3	2	0	1 lean meat
Spinach Dip	42	2	5	1	1 vegetable
Turkey Lettuce Wraps - 1 wrap	62	3	2	1	1/2 vegetable, 1 lean meat
GRAVIES & SAUCES					
Cornstarch Gravy	6	0	1	0	Free
Flour Gravy	9	0	2	0	Free
Fresh Cucumber Sauce for Seafood	37	3	3	0	1/2 vegetable, 1/2 fat
Fruit Sauce**	19	0	4	3	Free
Spanish Yogurt Sauce	27	0	4	0	1 vegetable
Thick and Chunky Salsa	14	0	3	1	Free
VEGETABLES					
Baked Portobello Mushrooms	32	1	4	1	1 vegetable
Basil Tomatoes	18	0	4	1	Free
Gourmet Cucumbers	23	0	5	1	1 vegetable
Gourmet Cucumbers**	14	0	3	1	Free
Italian Tomatoes	19	0	5	1	Free
Marinated Vegetables	19	1	3	1	Free
Seasoned Green Beans**	26	0	5	2	1 vegetable
SALADS					
Curry Tuna Salad	155	6	5	1	1 veget, 3 vl meat, 1/2 fat
Greek Salad	33	0	5	1	1 veget, 1/2 very lean meat
Shrimp Salad**	228	12 †	9	5 *	1 veget, 3 vl meat, 2 fat
POULTRY					
Chicken in Salsa	138	1	3	0	1 vegetable, 3 1/2 vl meat
Chicken Lettuce Wraps - 3 wraps	131	2	2	1	3 1/2 vl meat
Cooked and Cubed Chicken	108	1	0	0	3 vl meat
Grilled Chicken w/ Coconut-Cilantro**	165	4	3	0	1 vegetable, 3 1/2 vl meat
Hickory Smoked Barbecued Chicken	127	1	0	0	3 1/2 vl meat
Oven Fried Chicken	137	1	3	0	1/4 starch, 3 1/2 vl meat
Polynesian Chicken**	134	2	1	0	3 1/2 vl meat
Yogurt Cumin Chicken	143	2	5	0	1/3 fruit, 3 1/2 vl meat

	Calories	Total Fat Grams	Total Carb Grams	Dietary Fiber Grams	Food Exchanges
SEAFOOD					
Fillets of Sole Thermidor	146	3	3	0	3 1/2 vl meat
Fish in Salsa	128	2	3	0	1 vegetable, 3 vl meat
Grilled Salmon w/ Coconut-Cilantro**	202	10	3	0	1 vegetable, 3 lean meat
Hickory Smoked Barbecued Fish	164	7	0	0	3 lean meat
Lemon Fish	116	2	1	0	3 vl meat
Marinade: Lemon Basil	16	2	0	0	Free
Marinade: Soy	24	2	0	0	1/2 fat
Oven Fried Fish	134	2	5	0	1/3 starch, 3 vl meat
Poached Fish	120	2	1	0	3 vl meat
Polynesian Fish**	171	7	1	0	3 lean meat
Shrimp Lettuce Wraps - 3 wraps	129	1	4	1	3 vl meat
Shrimp Lettuce Wraps - 3 wraps**	121	1	2	1	3 vl meat
Sweet Mustard Fish**	131	2	2	0	1/2 vegetable, 3 vl meat
Tarragon Fish	146	3	2	0	1/4 milk, 3 vl meat
Yogurt Cumin Fish	132	2	5	0	1/3 fruit, 3 vl meat
BEEF AND PORK					
Marinated Steak	185	9	1	0	3 lean meat
Oven Fried Pork Loin	167	5	5	0	1/3 starch, 3 lean meat
GROUND MEAT AND SAUSAGE					
Beef Lettuce Wraps - 3 wraps	177	8	4	1	1 vegetable, 3 lean meat
Pizza Meat Loaf	187	9	2	0	1/2 vegetable, 3 lean meat
DESSERTS					
Cream Cheese Topping	29	1	3	0	1/3 milk

The following recipes are 1/2 Carb Serving for one portion.
6-10 grams of carbohydrates are counted as 1/2 Carb Serving.

	Calories	Total Fat Grams	Total Carb Grams	Dietary Fiber Grams	Food Exchanges
GRAVIES & SAUCES					
Fruit Sauce	32	0	8	3	1/2 fruit
SOUPS & STEWS					
Zero Vegetable Soup	35	0	6	2	1 vegetable
VEGETABLES					
Roasted Eggplant Medley	30	0	7	3	1 vegetable
Salsa Vegetables	30	0	7	1	1 vegetable
Seasoned Green Beans	28	0	6	2	1 vegetable
Zucchini, Tomato and Onion	29	0	7	2	1 vegetable

vl meat: very lean meat

*Fiber is 5 grams or more and has been subtracted from the total carbohydrate when figuring Carb Servings and Exchanges. **Indicates artificial sweetener used. This recipe is listed again without using artificial sweetener. † Most of the fat in this recipe is heart-healthy monosaturated and/or polyunsaturated fat.

1/2 Carb Serving, continued

	Calories	Total Fat Grams	Total Carb Grams	Dietary Fiber Grams	Food Exchanges
SALADS					
Apple Salad Mold	39	0	8	1	1/2 fruit
Broccoli Salad	68	4	6	3	1 vegetable, 1 fat
Cabbage Salad	52	2	9	3	2 vegetable
Cabbage Salad**	44	2	7	3	2 vegetable
Cinnamon Chicken Salad	169	5	10	1	1/2 fruit, 1 vegetable, 3 vl meat
Italian Garden Salad	58	4	6	1	1 vegetable, 1 fat
Mexican Garden Salad	119	10†	8	4	1 vegetable, 2 fat
Seafood Salad	85	3	7	0	1 vegetable, 1 lean meat
Shrimp Coleslaw	86	1	10	2	2 vegetable, 1 vl meat
Shrimp Coleslaw**	80	1	8	2	2 vegetable, 1 vl meat
Shrimp Salad	247	12†	14	5*	2 veget, 3 vl meat, 2 fat
Three Bean Salad	70	1	15	6*	1/2 starch, 1/2 vegetable
Three Bean Salad**	62	1	13	6*	1/2 starch, 1/2 vegetable
Vegetable Bean Salad**	44	0	9	4	1/3 starch, 1 vegetable
MEATLESS ENTREES					
Italian Zucchini Frittata	65	1	6	1	1 vegetable, 1 vl meat
Spanish Zucchini Frittata	59	0	7	2	1 vegetable, 1 vl meat
POULTRY					
Chicken and Broccoli Casserole	168	3	10	4	2 vegetable, 3 vl meat
Chicken Breasts Florentine	164	2	6	2	1 vegetable, 4 vl meat
Chicken Breasts in Mushroom Sauce	170	2	8	1	1/2 starch, 3 1/2 vl meat
Chicken Breasts Supreme	162	1	6	0	1/2 starch, 3 1/2 vl meat
Chicken Nuggets	164	1	9	0	2/3 starch, 3 1/2 vl meat
Chicken Picadillo	165	2	9	1	2 vegetable, 3 1/2 vl meat
Crispy Potato Chicken	167	3	6	1	1/2 starch, 3 1/2 vl meat
French Glazed Chicken	155	1	9	0	1/2 fruit, 3 1/2 vl meat
Grilled Chicken w/Coconut-Cilantro	178	4	7	0	1 vegetable, 3 1/2 vl meat
Grilled Chicken with Corn Salsa	154	2	7	1	1 vegetable, 3 1/2 vl meat
Grilled Chicken with Fruit Salsa	230	8†	13	5*	1/2 fruit, 3 1/2 vl meat, 1 fat
Rolled Chicken and Asparagus	151	2	6	3	1 vegetable, 3 1/2 vl meat
Teriyaki Chicken Stir-Fry	210	6†	10	3	2 vegetable, 3 1/2 vl meat, 1 fat
BEEF AND PORK					
Orange Pork Chops	210	7	10	1	1/2 fruit, 1 vegetable, 3 lean meat
Pork or Beef Stir-Fry	213	9	8	3	2 vegetable, 3 lean meat

vl meat: very lean meat

*Fiber is 5 grams or more and has been subtracted from the total carbohydrate when figuring Carb Servings and Exchanges. **Indicates artificial sweetener used. This recipe is listed again without using artificial sweetener. † Most of the fat in this recipe is heart-healthy monosaturated and/or polyunsaturated fat.

	Calories	Total Fat Grams	Total Carb Grams	Dietary Fiber Grams	Food Exchanges
SEAFOOD					
French Glazed Fish	145	2	9	0	1/2 fruit, 3 vl meat
Grilled Salmon with Fruit Salsa	264	14 †	12	5 *	1/2 fruit, 3 lean meat, 1 fat
Grilled Salmon w/Coconut-Cilantro	215	10 †	7	0	1 vegetable, 3 lean meat
Grilled Salmon with Corn Salsa	192	8 †	7	1	1 vegetable, 3 lean meat
Salmon Cakes	181	9	6	0	1/2 starch, 2 1/2 lean meat
Spanish Baked Fish	137	2	6	1	1 vegetable, 3 vl meat
Sweet Mustard Fish	162	2	10	0	1/2 starch, 1/2 vegetable, 3 vl meat
GROUND MEAT AND SAUSAGE					
Baked Meatballs	146	6	6	1	1/2 starch, 2 lean meat
Crustless Quiche	120	3	6	0	1/2 milk, 2 vl meat
Meat Patties	224	9	10	1	2/3 starch, 3 lean meat
Turkey Lettuce Wraps - 3 wraps	185	8	6	2	1 vegetable, 3 lean meat
DESSERTS					
Lemon Parfait	55	0	10	0	2/3 starch

The following recipes are 1 Carb Serving for one portion.
11-20 grams of carbohydrates are counted as 1 Carb Serving.

	Calories	Total Fat Grams	Total Carb Grams	Dietary Fiber Grams	Food Exchanges
BEVERAGES					
Banana Milk Shake**	99	0	20	1	1 fruit, 1/2 milk
Fruit Milk Shake	96	0	19	2	1 fruit, 1/2 milk
Fruit Milk Shake**	80	0	14	2	1/2 fruit, 1/2 milk
Juice Cooler	56	0	13	0	1 fruit
BREADS					
Cottage Cheese Pancakes**	119	1	17	3	1 starch, 1 vl meat
Dumplings	85	0	17	2	1 starch
Italian Focaccia Bread	104	1	20	1	1 starch
Oat Bran Muffins	121	4	20	3	1 starch
SOUPS & STEWS					
Chili Con Carne	242	6	27	11 *	1/2 starch, 2 vegetable, 2 lean meat
Chilled Tomato-Shrimp Soup	129	1	11	1	2 vegetable, 2 vl meat
French Onion Soup	138	3	18	2	1 starch, 1 lean meat
Gazpacho	91	3	16	3	3 vegetable, 1/2 fat
Minestrone Soup	110	1	20	5 *	3/4 starch, 1 vegetable
Oriental Noodle Soup	79	1	14	1	2/3 starch, 1 vegetable
Three Bean Soup	126	1	26	8 *	1 starch, 1 vegetable

1 Carb Serving, continued

	Calories	Total Fat Grams	Total Carb Grams	Dietary Fiber Grams	Food Exchanges
POTATOES, RICE and BEANS					
Cheese Stuffed Potatoes	71	0	12	2	1 starch
Sweet Potato Fries	116	4	20	3	1 1/2 starch, 1/2 fat
SALADS					
Chicken and Fruit Salad	171	3	19	3	1 fruit, 1 vegetable, 2 1/2 vl meat
Chicken and Spinach Salad	190	7	16	4	1 fruit, 2 1/2 lean meat
Fruit Salad	60	0	14	1	1 starch
Grapefruit & Avocado Salad	134	8†	16	5*	1/2 fruit, 1 vegetable, 1 1/2 fat
Grapefruit & Avocado Salad**	128	8†	14	5*	1/2 fruit, 1 vegetable, 1 1/2 fat
Herb Potato Salad	72	1	14	2	1 starch
Lime Cottage Salad	121	1	16	0	1/2 fruit, 1/2 milk, 1 vl meat
Macaroni Salad**	134	5	19	2	1 starch, 1 vegetable, 1 fat
Pear Salad with Raspberry Dressing	196	11†	24	5	1 fruit, 1 vegetable, 2 fat
Romaine & Mandarin Orange Salad	286	22†	22	8*	1 fruit, 1 hf meat, 3 fat
Romaine & Mandarin Orange Salad**	272	22†	19	8*	2/3 fruit, 1 hf meat, 3 fat
Romaine Salad w/ Berries, Maple Nuts	222	17†	17	4	2/3 fruit, 1 vegetable, 3 1/2 fat
Vegetable Bean Salad	52	0	11	4	1/3 starch, 1 vegetable
SANDWICHES & PIZZA					
Individual Pizza	167	4	18	3	1 starch, 1/2 vegetable, 1 1/2 lean meat
Tomato and Ricotta Sandwich	148	4	19	3	1 starch, 1 vegetable, 1 lean meat
POULTRY					
Chicken and Pea Pod Stir-fry	188	2	14	4	3 vegetable, 3 vl meat
Chicken and Vegetables in Gravy	192	2	11	4	1/2 starch, 1 vegetable, 3 1/2 vl meat
Chicken Cacciatore	197	2	15	4	1/2 starch, 2 vegetable, 3 1/2 vl meat
Mandarin Orange Chicken	187	2	15	3	1/3 fruit, 2 vegetable, 3 1/2 vl meat
Polynesian Chicken	186	2	14	0	1 starch, 3 1/2 vl meat
Spicy Chicken and Grapes	172	1	17	2	3/4 fruit, 1 veget, 3 vl meat
Spicy Chicken and Grapes**	162	1	15	2	3/4 fruit, 1 veget, 3 vl meat
Sweet and Sour Chicken**	152	1	12	2	1/2 fruit, 1 veget, 3 vl meat
SEAFOOD					
Mandarin Orange Seafood	163	1	17	3	1/3 fruit, 2 veget, 3 vl meat
Oven Fried Oysters	110	2	13	0	1 starch, 1 vl meat
Polynesian Fish	223	7	14	0	1 starch, 3 lean meat

	Calories	Total Fat Grams	Total Carb Grams	Dietary Fiber Grams	Food Exchanges
BEEF AND PORK					
Chinese Pepper Steak	253	9	16	3	2 veget, 2 1/2 lean meat
Chinese Pepper Steak**	251	9	16	3	2 veget, 2 1/2 lean meat
Italian Pork Skillet	198	5	12	4	2 vegetable, 3 lean meat
Pork Chop Suey	219	5	16	2	1/3 starch, 2 vegetable, 3 lean meat
GROUND MEAT AND SAUSAGE					
Asparagus Topped Meatloaf	286	10	19	4	1 starch, 1 vegetable, 3 lean meat
Barbecued Smoked Sausage & Cabbage Casserole	203	8	17	3	1/2 starch, 2 vegetable, 2 lean meat
Meat Loaf	244	9	16	2	2/3 starch, 1 vegetable, 3 lean meat
Sausage and Sauerkraut	230	8	22	6*	2/3 starch, 1 vegetable, 2 lean meat
Swedish Meatballs	214	8	13	2	2/3 starch, 3 lean meat
DESSERTS					
Apple Cake**	110	4	17	2	1 starch, 1/2 fat
Apple Crisp	88	1	19	2	1/2 starch, 1/2 fruit
Apple Crisp**	68	1	14	2	1/2 starch, 2/3 fruit
Chocolate Mocha Mousse	104	0	20	1	1 1/3 starch
Coffee Mousse	96	0	18	0	1 starch
Fruit Slush	91	0	17	4	1/2 fruit, 1/2 milk
Fruit Slush**	74	0	13	4	1/2 fruit, 1/2 milk
Mandarin Orange Cake**	112	3	18	1	1 1/3 starch
Peppermint Mousse	102	0	19	0	1 starch
White Chocolate Mousse with Berries	78	0	16	2	1 starch

hf meat: high fat meat   **vl meat:** very lean meat

*Fiber is 5 grams or more and has been subtracted from the total carbohydrate when figuring Carb Servings and Exchanges. **Indicates artificial sweetener used. This recipe is listed again without using artificial sweetener. † Most of the fat in this recipe is heart-healthy monosaturated and/or polyunsaturated fat.

The following recipes are 1 1/2 Carb Servings for one portion.

21-25 grams of carbohydrates are counted as 1 1/2 Carb Servings.

	Calories	Total Fat Grams	Total Carb Grams	Dietary Fiber Grams	Food Exchanges
BEVERAGES					
Banana Milk Shake	115	0	24	1	1 fruit, 1/2 milk
Orange Julius	113	0	22	0	1 fruit, 1/2 milk
BREADS					
Applesauce Oatmeal Coffee Cake	153	4	25	2	1 1/2 starch, 1/2 fat
Blueberry Coffee Cake	146	4	24	2	1 1/2 starch, 1/2 fat
Cottage Cheese Pancakes	135	1	22	3	1 1/2 starch, 1 vl meat
Refrigerator Bran Muffins	142	5	25	4	1 1/2 starch, 1/2 fat
SOUPS & STEWS					
Italian Cioppino	207	2	22	4	4 vegetable, 3 vl meat
Mulligatawny Soup	248	2	24	2	1 starch, 1/2 fruit, 4 vl meat
New England Fish Chowder	220	2	22	2	1 starch, 1/2 milk, 3 vl meat
Thai Chicken Soup	227	5	21	3	1 starch, 1 vegetable, 2 1/2 lean meat
POTATOES, RICE and BEANS					
Herb Rice Blend	132	1	25	2	1 1/2 starch
Low-Fat French Fries	129	4	22	3	1 1/2 starch, 1/2 fat
Ranch Beans	160	0	31	9*	1 1/2 starch
Roasted Root Vegetables	131	4	23	4	1 starch, 1 veget, 1/2 fat
Scalloped Potatoes	107	0	22	3	1 1/2 starch
SALADS					
Chinese Chicken Salad	210	6	24	3	1 starch, 2 vegetable, 1 lean meat, 1/2 fat
Chinese Chicken Salad**	205	6	22	3	1 starch, 2 vegetable, 1 lean meat, 1/2 fat
Macaroni Salad	141	5	21	2	1 starch, 1 veget, 1 fat
MEATLESS ENTREES					
Italian Broccoli and Pasta	109	1	22	3	1 starch, 1 1/2 vegetable
Puffy Chile Relleno Casserole	290	10	21	3	1 starch, 1 vegetable, 3 lean meat
Vegetables Primavera	169	3	29	5*	1 starch, 2 vegetable
POULTRY					
Chicken and Artichokes Dijon	316	7	28	5*	1 starch, 1 vegetable, 3 1/2 vl meat, 1/2 fat
Chicken and Artichokes Dijon**	308	7	26	5*	1 starch, 1 vegetable, 3 1/2 vl meat, 1/2 fat
Chicken and Rice Casserole	247	2	25	4	1 starch, 2 veget, 3 vl meat
Mediterranean Chicken	213	2	25	3	1 1/3 starch, 1 vegetable, 2 1/2 vl meat
Mexican Style Chicken and Rice	241	4	25	3	1 starch, 2 veget, 3 vl meat
Sweet and Sour Chicken	193	1	23	2	1 fruit, 1 veget, 3 vl meat

	Calories	Total Fat Grams	Total Carb Grams	Dietary Fiber Grams	Food Exchanges
SEAFOOD					
Spicy Seafood with Grapes	192	1	24	2	1 fruit, 1 veget, 3 vl meat
Spicy Seafood with Grapes**	179	1	21	2	1 fruit, 1 veget, 3 vl meat
BEEF AND PORK					
Fajitas Barbecue Style	328	10	25	4	1 1/2 starch, 1 vegetable, 3 lean meat
GROUND MEAT AND SAUSAGE					
Quick Meat and Bean Supper	296	8	27	6*	1 starch, 1 vegetable, 3 lean meat
DESSERTS					
Apple Cake	142	4	25	2	1 1/2 starch, 1/2 fat
Butterfly Cup Cakes	140	4	23	1	1 1/2 starch, 1/2 fat
Cream Cheese Dessert	181	6	25	1	1 fruit, 1 milk, 1 fat
Fruit Pizza For A Crowd	166	6	24	1	1 starch, 1/2 fruit, 1 fat
Grasshopper Mousse	115	0	22	0	1 1/2 starch
Mandarin Orange Cake	134	3	24	1	1 1/2 starch
Pineapple Cake**	96	0	21	1	1 starch, 1/2 fruit
Strawberries Romanoff	100	0	22	3	1/2 starch, 1 fruit

The following recipes are 2 Carb Servings for one portion.
26-35 grams of carbohydrates are counted as 2 Carb Servings.

	Calories	Total Fat Grams	Total Carb Grams	Dietary Fiber Grams	Food Exchanges
SOUPS & STEWS					
Quick & Healthy Tortilla Soup	248	3	40	8*	2 starch, 1 veget, 2 vl meat
Sausage and Bean Soup	261	6	38	12*	1 1/3 starch, 1 vegetable, 2 lean meat
Taco Soup	285	6	40	10*	1 starch, 3 vegetable, 2 lean meat
POTATOES, RICE and BEANS					
Herb and Vegetable Rice Blend	136	1	26	2	1 1/2 starch, 1 vegetable
SALADS					
Oriental Rice and Seafood Salad	229	2	29	3	1 1/2 starch, 1 vegetable, 2 1/2 vl meat
Oriental Rice and Seafood Salad**	219	2	26	3	1 1/2 starch, 1 vegetable, 2 1/2 vl meat

vl meat: very lean meat

*Fiber is 5 grams or more and has been subtracted from the total carbohydrate when figuring Carb Servings and Exchanges. **Indicates artificial sweetener used. This recipe is listed again without using artificial sweetener. † Most of the fat in this recipe is heart-healthy monosaturated and/or polyunsaturated fat.

2 Carb Servings, continued

	Calories	Total Fat Grams	Total Carb Grams	Dietary Fiber Grams	Food Exchanges
SANDWICHES & PIZZA					
Boboli Pizza - Sausage Style	244	8	26	1	1 1/2 starch, 1/2 vegetable, 1 1/2 medium fat meat
Boboli Pizza - Shrimp Style	259	6	28	1	1 1/2 starch, 1 vegetable, 2 lean meat
Crusty Calzone	237	7	30	3	2 starch, 1 1/2 lean meat
Meatball Sandwich	331	10	40	6*	2 starch, 1 vegetable, 2 lean meat
Piled High Vegetable Pizza	252	7	34	5*	1 1/2 starch, 2 vegetables, 1 medium fat meat
Sloppy Joes	321	10	31	4	2 starch, 3 lean meat
Turkey French Dips	271	8	31	4	2 starch, 2 lean meat
MEATLESS ENTREES					
Quick Lasagne	218	5	28	2	1 1/2 starch, 1 vegetable, 1 lean meat
POULTRY					
Baked Chimichangas	260	5	27	2	1 1/2 starch, 1 vegetable, 2 1/2 vl meat
Chicken and Biscuits	257	3	32	4	1 1/2 starch, 1 vegetable, 3 vl meat
Chicken Enchiladas	237	6	26	3	1 1/2 starch, 1 vegetable, 2 vl meat
Chicken Fajitas	278	3	30	3	1 2/3 starch, 1 vegetable, 3 1/2 vl meat
Chicken Tortilla Casserole	274	6	30	3	2 starch, 3 vl meat
Green Chile Chicken Enchilada Casserole	281	8	27	2	1 starch, 2 vegetable, 3 lean meat
SEAFOOD					
Mediterranean Seafood	201	1	28	3	1 1/2 starch, 1 vegetable, 2 vl meat
BEEF AND PORK					
Beef or Pork Fajitas	332	10	30	3	1 2/3 starch, 1 vegetable, 3 lean meat
Pork and Rice Casserole	291	8	27	3	1 1/2 starch, 1 vegetable, 3 lean meat

vl meat: very lean meat

*Fiber is 5 grams or more and has been subtracted from the total carbohydrate when figuring Carb Servings and Exchanges. **Indicates artificial sweetener used. This recipe is listed again without using artificial sweetener. † Most of the fat in this recipe is heart-healthy monosaturated and/or polyunsaturated fat.

	Calories	Total Fat Grams	Total Carb Grams	Dietary Fiber Grams	Food Exchanges
GROUND MEAT AND SAUSAGE					
Bean and Beef/Turkey Enchiladas	330	9	41	9*	1 2/3 starch, 1 vegetable, 2 1/2 lean meat
Biscuits and Gravy	292	11	28	1	2 starch, 2 lean meat, 1 fat
Creamy Cabbage Stir-fry	340	10	37	5*	1 1/2 starch, 2 vegetable, 3 lean meat
John Torrey	238	7	26	3	1 starch, 2 vegetable, 2 lean meat
Moore	309	9	33	1	2 starch, 1 vegetable, 2 1/2 lean meat
Quick Meat Lasagne	265	7	29	2	1 1/2 starch, 1 vegetable, 2 lean meat
Smoked Sausage & Rice Casserole	288	9	33	3	1 2/3 starch, 1 vegetable, 2 lean meat
Spaghetti and Meatballs	277	9	28	4	1 1/4 starch, 2 vegetable, 2 lean meat
Tortilla Pie	262	8	28	3	1 starch, 2 vegetable, 2 lean meat
DESSERTS					
Pineapple Cake	121	0	28	1	1 1/4 starch, 1/2 fruit

The following recipes are 2 1/2 Carb Servings for one portion.
36-40 grams of carbohydrates are counted as 2 1/2 Carb Servings.

	Calories	Total Fat Grams	Total Carb Grams	Dietary Fiber Grams	Food Exchanges
Tomato and Basil Pasta	193	1	39	4	2 starch, 2 vegetable
Clam Fettucini	273	2	39	2	2 1/2 starch, 2 vl meat

The following recipes are 3 Carb Servings for one portion.
41-50 grams of carbohydrates are counted as 3 Carb Servings.

	Calories	Total Fat Grams	Total Carb Grams	Dietary Fiber Grams	Food Exchanges
Chicken in a Pocket	367	6	49	3	3 starch, 3 vl meat
Chocolate Cake	273	10	45	2	3 starch, 1 fat

Dietary Fiber

High fiber foods should be part of your daily diet. Research has found that dietary fiber helps to lower cholesterol, improves blood sugar control and protects against certain colon problems.

There are two types of dietary fiber:

Insoluble Fiber: This type of fiber is found in wheat bran, whole grains and vegetables. It does not dissolve in water but instead absorbs water. It provides bulk to stools and helps with bowel elimination. Studies indicate that this fiber may help to prevent problems associated with the colon such as:

> constipation
> diverticulosis
> hemorrhoids
> colon and rectal cancer

Soluble Fiber: This type of fiber is found in oats, legumes such as beans and peas, and some grains. It is also added to processed foods as pectin and guar gums. It becomes a gel when mixed with water. Studies indicate that this fiber helps with:

> lowering cholesterol by interfering with its production
> improving blood sugar control by slowing the absorption of glucose

How much fiber do you need?
Your goal should be to consume at least 25 grams of dietary fiber everyday. A real challenge for most people!

The best sources of fiber are whole grains, fruits, vegetables, beans and nuts.
Fiber is significantly reduced when fruits and vegetables are peeled and when grains are refined through processing.

Foods with 2.5 - 4.9 grams of fiber are considered a good source.
Foods with 5 or more grams of fiber are considered an excellent source.

Sources of Dietary Fiber
Following is a listing of fiber sources and the approximate total grams of dietary fiber for the serving size listed. Use this as a guide but be sure to read labels on packaged foods as the amount of fiber will vary with different brands.

Sources of Dietary Fiber

Cereals	fiber grams
All-Bran Buds, 1/3 cup	13
Bran Flakes, 3/4 cup	5
Cheerios, 1 cup	3
Fiber One, 1/2 cup	14
Frosted Mini-Wheats, 1 cup	6
Fruit & Fiber, 1 cup	5
Oatbran, 1 1/4 cups cooked	6
Oatmeal, 1 cup cooked	4
Oatmeal, instant, 1 packet	3
Raisin Bran, 1 cup	7
Shredded Wheat, 2 biscuits	5
Total, whole grain, 3/4 cup	3
Wheaties, 1 cup	3

Grains, Rice and Pasta	
Whole wheat English muffin	4
Whole grain bread, 1 ounce	3
Brown rice, 1/2 cup cooked	2
Barley, 1/2 cup cooked	3
Bulgur, 1/2 cup cooked	4
Spaghetti noodles, 1 cup cooked	2
Popcorn, 3 cups	3

Vegetables	
Asparagus, 1 cup cooked	3
Beets, 1/2 cup cooked	2
Broccoli, 1/2 cup cooked	3
Brussels sprouts, 1/2 cup cooked	2
Cauliflower, 1/2 cup cooked	2
Cabbage, 1/2 cup cooked	2
Carrots, 1/2 cup cooked	3
Corn, 1/2 cup cooked	2
Cucumber with peel, 1 medium	2
Eggplant, 1 cup cooked	3
Green beans, 1/2 cup cooked	2
Bell pepper, 1 medium raw	2
Potato, with skin – 1 medium	4
Snow peas, 1 cup raw	2
Spinach, 1/2 cup cooked	2
Summer squash, 1 cup cooked	3
Sweet potato, 1/2 cup cooked	3
Winter squash, 1/2 cup cooked	3

Dried Beans, & Legumes	fiber grams
Black beans, 1/2 cup cooked	8
Garbanzo, 1/2 cup cooked	6
Kidney beans, 1/2 cup cooked	6
Lentils, 1/2 cup cooked	8
Lima beans, 1/2 cup cooked	6
Pinto beans, 1/2 cup cooked	7
Peas, 1/2 cup cooked	4
Refried beans, fat-free, 1/2 cup	6
Split peas, 1/2 cup cooked	8

Fruits	
Apple with skin, 1 medium	4
Apricots, 5	4
*Avocado, 1 medium	9
Banana, 1 medium	3
Blueberries, 1 cup	4
Cherries, 1 cup	3
Grapefruit, 1 medium	3
Grapes, seedless, 1 cup	2
Kiwi, 1 medium	3
Nectarine, 1 medium	2
Orange, 1 medium	3
Peach, 1 medium	2
Pear, 1 medium	4
Pineapple, 1 cup	2
Plums, 2	2
Prunes, dried, 5	3
Raisins, 1/4 cup	2
Raspberries, 1 cup	8
Strawberries, 1 cup	3

*Nuts/Seeds, dry roasted	
Almonds, 24 nuts (1 ounce)	3
Cashews, 18 nuts (1 ounce)	1
Filberts (hazelnuts), 20 nuts	3
Flaxseeds, 1 tablespoon	3
Peanuts, 28 nuts (1 ounce)	2
Pistachios, 47 nuts (1 ounce)	3
Soy nuts, 1/4 cup (1 1/2 ounces)	3
Sunflower seeds, kernels, (1 ounce)	3
Walnuts - 14 halves (1 ounce)	2
Peanut butter, 2 tablespoons	2

*Although these foods are higher in fat, most of the fat is healthy monosaturated and polyunsaturated.

Go Nuts!

Once thought of as a high fat food and one to avoid, nuts are now recommended as part of a healthy diet.

Current research has found that including one ounce of nuts in your daily diet may reduce the risk of heart disease, diabetes and some forms of cancer.

Nuts contain little saturated fat, are cholesterol-free and are a good source of heart-healthy monosaturated and polyunsaturated fats. In addition, most nuts are a good source of fiber, protein, antioxidants, phytosterols and many vitamins and minerals.

The fact that nuts provide satiety, which means that nuts help to make you feel full longer, makes them a good choice for a snack. The trick is limiting the amount you eat to only one ounce a day. Add nuts in moderation, without adding extra fat or calories, by substituting for other snacks. Studies have shown that one ounce of nuts, when included as part of a low-fat diet, does not cause weight gain.

What is one ounce of nuts?

Almonds	20-24
Brazil nuts	6-8
Cashews	16-18
Hazelnuts (filberts)	18-20
Macadamia nuts	10-12
Peanuts	28
Pecans	18-20 halves
Pistachios	45-47
Walnuts	8-11 halves

Several recipes in this book use nuts in moderation. These recipes have a higher fat content and contain the following notation: *Most of the fat in this recipe is heart-healthy monosaturated and/or polyunsaturated fat.*

Refer to the section titled "All Fats Are Not Equal" to learn more about heart-healthy fats.

All Fats Are Not Equal

The type of fat you include in your diet is just as important as the amounts you include. However, your intake of fat should be no more than 30% of your total calories.

Monosaturated fats - the best choice
> Sources: canola oil, olive oil, peanut oil, avocado, olives, almonds, cashews, peanuts, pecans and sesame seeds

---

Omega-3 fats - another best choice
> This is a type of polyunsaturated fat.
> Sources: fish such as salmon

Polyunsaturated fats - a good choice
> Sources: soybean oil, corn oil, sunflower oil, English walnuts, sunflower seeds, and many salad dressings

---

Saturated fats - should be limited
> Sources: dairy products such as cheese, butter and milk; meats, coconut, palm or palm kernel oil, cocoa butter and hardened shortenings

---

Trans fats - should be avoided
> Sources: commercially prepared foods such as chips, cookies, crackers and muffins; foods that list hydrogenated or partially hydrogenated on the label

Trans fats are formed when a liquid oil is hardened by the process called hydrogenation. When buying margarine look for the label that states *no trans fats*.

Both trans fats and saturated fats are known to increase blood levels of cholesterol. In contrast, both monosaturated fats and polyunsaturated fats are known to lower blood cholesterol levels when they are part of a low-fat diet.

Tips for Reducing
Fat and Cholesterol in Your Diet

Limiting fat and cholesterol in your diet is important whether your goal is to lose weight, lower your cholesterol or just be more healthy. Here are some ideas to help.

Substitute low-fat snacks for high-fat snacks and limit the amount you eat. Look for no more than 3 grams of fat for every 100 calories.

- one ounce of nuts*
- fresh fruit
- fat-free hot cocoa
- low-fat frozen yogurt
- low-fat ice milk
- low-fat crackers and cookies
- rice cakes
- frozen juice bars
- unsalted-top saltines
- air-popped popcorn
- pretzels, both hard and soft
- tomato juice with a twist of lemon
- corn cakes (caramel flavor is a favorite)
- fruit slices served with nonfat yogurt for dipping
- graham crackers, vanilla wafers, gingersnaps, animal crackers, fig bars
- soda pop with a scoop of low-fat ice milk (use diet pop to reduce calories)
- light microwave popcorn - butter flavor or kettle corn
- raw vegetable sticks with low-fat ranch dressing for a dip

* Nuts are a good choice because they contain heart-healthy monosaturated and/or polyunsaturated fat. Limit to one ounce a day.

Change how you prepare foods:
- Remove the skin from chicken.
- Remove fat from homemade and canned soups.
- Bake, broil, simmer, microwave or barbecue.
- Cook foods in a few tablespoons of broth, fruit juice or water.
- When frying foods, use non-stick cooking spray or use a spray pump.

Substitute the following low-fat or nonfat foods for higher-fat foods:

> nonfat or 1% milk
> evaporated skim milk
> nonfat yogurt (plain or flavored)
> ice milk
> light, reduced-fat, or nonfat sour cream
> light, reduced-fat, or nonfat cream cheese
> low-fat, reduced-fat, or nonfat mayonnaise
> low-fat, reduced-fat, or nonfat salad dressings
> low-fat or reduced-fat cheeses
> low-fat or reduced-fat margarine
> water-packed tuna

Avoid or limit the following foods:

> High-fat meats such as bacon, bologna and salami
> Foods fried in oil, lard or other fats
> Fried snack foods such as potato chips, corn chips and cheese curls
> Pastries, cookies and rich desserts
> Foods with trans fats *(these are foods that list hydrogenated or partially hydrogenated as one of the first ingredients)*

Choose:

> only lean meats and cut off all fat before cooking.
> lean beef with 7% fat or less.
> ground turkey with 7% fat or less.
> meat that has little or no marbling of fat.
> an egg substitute to limit egg yolks - or use two egg whites in place of one egg.
> a sprinkle of imitation butter flavor sprinkles instead of margarine on vegetables.
> a fruit spread or nonfat cream cheese on toast instead of margarine.
> lettuce and tomato on sandwiches and leave off the mayonnaise.
> a margarine that does not have trans fatty acids.

Most fruits and vegetables are fat-free and are good low-calorie, high-fiber choices. Your higher fat foods are often processed foods such as fried foods, frozen breaded products, cookies, pastries, chips and fast foods. Cutting back on fat and eating more fruits and vegetables is also a good way to lose weight.

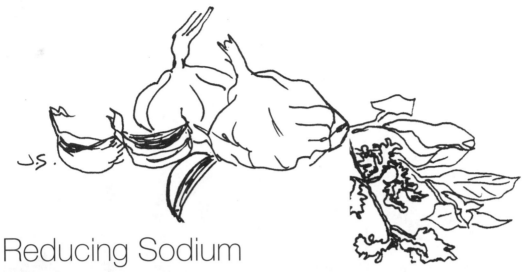

Reducing Sodium

Not everyone needs to be on a sodium restricted diet.
However, it is still prudent to limit sodium to no more than 2400 milligrams (mg) per day. If you are on a sodium restricted diet, you may find it helpful to seek guidance from a registered dietitian.

The three best ways to cut back on sodium are:

Don't use salt at the table.

Use less salt in cooking. Keep in mind that a small amount used in cooking may give just enough flavor to help you from adding too much at the table.

Avoid processed foods. These are convenience foods, canned foods, fast foods and most snack foods. Processed foods usually have salt added and have more sodium than fresh foods.

If you are trying to reduce the sodium in your diet, here are some additional guidelines to help you:

Use fresh foods in place of processed foods when possible.

Buy canned vegetables with no added salt.

Drain and rinse vegetables canned with salt.

Don't eat salted and cured meats such as ham, bacon and luncheon meats.

Try some of the lower sodium products such as reduced-salt ham or reduced-salt bacon. These still have large amounts of sodium but less than the real thing.

Use salt-free or reduced-salt soups, broth and bouillon.

Go light on condiments such as ketchup, mustard and steak sauce.

Add vinegar or a lemon or lime slice to your plate to flavor fish and vegetables such as spinach.

Use seasoning powders and do not use seasoning salts. Garlic powder is a better choice than garlic salt.

Learn to use herbs and spices in cooking to add flavor. Herbs and spices are not a significant source of sodium.

Try unsalted snack foods such as: unsalted, baked tortilla chips; unsalted popcorn; whole grain crackers with unsalted tops.

Make fast foods lower in sodium by ordering hamburgers without pickles and cheese. Order French fries without salt.

Note: Salt is listed as an optional ingredient in the recipes in this book and is therefore not included in the nutrient analysis of the recipes. When possible, canned products without the addition of salt, or reduced-salt were used.

Ten Steps to Weight Loss

If your goal is to lose weight, try some of these helpful ideas:

1. Plan

Plan meals before shopping.
Make a grocery list.
Grocery shop when you are NOT hungry.
Do not buy high calorie foods that you will
  be too tempted to eat.

2. Make Better Food Choices

Choose low-fat foods and high fiber foods.
Use less fat in cooking.
Try recipes that are low-fat and low-calorie.
Use less foods high in saturated fats.
Avoid foods with trans fats.
Replace saturated fats and trans fats with
  monosaturated and poylunsaturated fats.

3. Eat less

Eat a smaller amount. This is just as important as what you eat.
Cook only the amount you need if you are tempted by leftovers.
Use a smaller plate so it will not look empty.

4. Control snacking

Have healthy snacks on hand. Examples: fresh fruit,
  vegetables, diet soda pop
Try one ounce of nuts.
Limit how often you snack and eat smaller amounts.
Ask yourself if you are hungry. Only eat if hungry.

5. Keep food out of sight

Never leave food on the counter.
Store it out of sight in a cupboard.
Put tempting food in hard to reach places.

6. Don't eat just for something to do

Find a hobby you enjoy.
Go for a walk.
Call or visit a friend.
Do volunteer work.
Get a job.

7. Change your eating habits

Make a list of your bad eating habits.
Write down what you can do to change each bad habit.
Practice good eating habits.

8. Set a goal you can reach

A one to two pound loss per week is good.
Choose a weight goal that is good for you.
You don't have to be skinny.

9. Exercise

Exercise at least 4-5 times a week or
    better yet, everyday.
Find a friend to walk with.
Choose a time of the day that is
    good for you.

10. Enjoy eating

Eat slowly and enjoy each bite.
Do not drink when there is
    food in your mouth.
Do nothing else while eating
    so you can enjoy each bite.
Put your fork down while
    chewing and only pick it up when your mouth is empty.
A smaller amount of food eaten slowly can be more enjoyable
    than a large amount eaten fast.

Exercise - Get Going!

Exercising for 20-30 minutes everyday should be your goal. However, exercising just four to five times a week is also very good. Anything you do to get your body moving is better than doing nothing at all. Some of the popular aerobic exercises - exercise that uses oxygen - are walking, jogging, aerobic classes, jumping rope and use of special equipment such as a stair stepper, cross country machine and treadmill.

The benefits of exercise:

        lowers risk of heart disease

        increases good cholesterol

        improves blood pressure

        lowers risk of osteoporosis

        improves blood sugar control

        increases basal metabolic rate

        helps with weight loss

        lowers body fat

        improves quality of life

        improves mental health and reduces depression

Here are some ideas to get you started:

Do what you enjoy.
If you enjoy what you are doing, there is a better chance you will continue.

Get a routine going.
Plan to exercise at least five times a week. If you miss one time you will still have exercised four times. Exercising on a regular basis becomes a routine - like brushing your teeth.

Find a time that works for you.
Look at your daily schedule and see what time of the day is good for you.

Ask friends to join you.
Exercising with friends will make the time go by faster and it's more fun.

Have a back-up plan.
If you won't walk in the rain, plan to walk in a mall or go to a health club. If you go to exercise classes and know you will miss one, plan on doing another kind of exercise at a better time for you.

Wear the right shoes and clothing.
If you walk for exercise, you'll need good walking shoes and a raincoat. Sweat suits or shorts are fine for health clubs. You don't have to buy expensive clothes.

Don't put off exercising until tomorrow.
Remember, tomorrow never comes.

Add extra steps throughout your day.
Park the car further away, use stairs instead of elevators and walk during your break time. Every little bit counts.

You are important.
Your health, both physical and mental, is important. It's okay to take time for yourself to exercise or just to relax. Don't feel guilty!

Think positive and you will succeed!

Note: It is very important to consult a physician before starting any exercise program.

Time Saving Ideas

Listed below are some ideas to help you save time in the kitchen:

Take advantage of produce that is cleaned, sliced and/or peeled. Although these may cost more, it is worth it if lack of time is keeping you from eating fresh vegetables.

Buy whole vegetables, including lettuce, that have not been cleaned or sliced. Save time by cleaning and slicing the vegetables, all at one time, and then refrigerate in resealable plastic bags. This will be less expensive.

A salad spinner is a must to make cleaning lettuce a quick task. Do a whole head of lettuce and store in resealable plastic bags. I prefer this type of lettuce over the packages of pre-washed lettuce.

Use alfalfa sprouts in sandwiches and salads. These are ready to use right from the container. No chopping!

Buy packages of stir-fry vegetables and meat or poultry ready cut for stir-frying.

Stock your freezer with foods that thaw quickly for last minute meals. An example is packages of individually frozen skinned and boned chicken breasts.

To skin chicken parts, place a paper towel on the skin and pull.

Purchase packaged cornflake crumbs, instead of crushing cornflakes, for use in breading meats. These are usually found with the breadings in the grocery store.

Use quick-cooking brown rice. It cooks in only 10 minutes!

Chopping cilantro can be simplified. Save time and reduce spoilage by chopping a bunch at one time and freezing for future use.

> Wash a bunch of cilantro with the stems tied together. Shake off water. Start chopping from the leafy end - on a cutting board - and stop chopping when you reach mostly stems. A French knife works well for this task. Freeze in resealable plastic bags. Small amounts can easily be removed as needed.

Fresh herbs always taste the best, but dried herbs also work well. When buying fresh, chop all at one time and freeze in resealable plastic bags for future use.

The taste of fresh minced ginger is hard to replace. Save time by mincing all at one time and freezing in resealable plastic bags. Or freeze the ginger whole and grate the amount you need, while frozen.

Purchase chopped or minced garlic and substitute it for fresh. It's available in the produce section. This saves time chopping.

Use dried onion instead of chopping fresh. See the label for reconstituting.

Marinate foods in a resealable plastic bag. This eliminates extra clean-up. Always marinate meat, poultry and seafood in the refrigerator.

Keep staple foods on hand so that you always have the ingredients for several meals.

Organize your grocery list in categories so you will be less likely to miss an item. Find a convenient place in your kitchen for the list and encourage family members to add to it. Ask them to add items when they are low and not empty.

Plan meals for the next week and add items needed to the grocery list before shopping.

Grocery shop from your list once a week and avoid stops at the grocery store after work.

Plan on leftovers. Double a recipe and freeze for future meals or freeze in individual portions for lunch.

Quick Breakfast Ideas

**A good breakfast gives you a jump-start for the day.
It provides energy as well as valuable nutrients.**

Include some of the following for a healthy breakfast:

Protein-rich foods - Choose those low in fat such as lean meats, low-fat cheeses and egg substitute (or eggs within recommended amount).

Fresh fruit or fruit juice - Fresh fruit is a better choice as it provides more fiber than juice.

Whole grain breads and cereals - These add fiber to your diet.

Low-fat dairy products - Choose nonfat milk or yogurt.

Listed are some breakfast ideas that do not require a recipe:

Hot Cereal
Cook oatmeal or oat bran cereal. Top with nonfat or low-fat yogurt and fruit.

Cold Cereal
Serve whole grain cereal with nonfat milk and fresh fruit. Look for cereal with less than 3 grams of fat per serving and at least 3 grams of fiber per serving.

Peanut Butter
Spread on whole grain toast.

Bagel
Top a whole grain bagel with nonfat or low-fat cream cheese or a low–fat spreadable cheese.

Yogurt and Fruit
Add fruit to nonfat or low-fat yogurt. Fresh berries work well and add fiber. Serve with whole grain toast.

Breakfast Yogurt
Mix nonfat or low-fat yogurt with fresh fruit. Add a high fiber cereal.

Breakfast Pizza
Toast a whole grain English muffin half.
Top with pizza sauce (or tomato sauce or chili sauce) and part-skim mozzarella cheese. Heat under broiler until cheese is melted.

Omelets
Make an omelet and top with salsa. Egg substitute works well in omelets. Add cooked mushrooms or other vegetables. This is a good way to use leftover vegetables.

Low-fat Cooking
Use non-stick cooking spray for cooking tortillas, pancakes, French toast and eggs or egg substitute.

Reduce Fat
Try whole wheat toast with sugar–free jam and leave off the margarine.

Low-Sugar
Use sugar-free jam on pancakes or French toast. Unsweetened applesauce is also good on pancakes.

Cheese and Fruit
Serve low-fat cottage cheese or low–fat ricotta cheese with fruit. Add whole grain toast.

Quick Sandwiches Ideas

Listed below are some sandwich ideas for variety, saving time and cutting calories and fat.

Add moisture

Cut back on calories by using a low-fat mayonnaise, spread thinly.
Or leave off the mayonnaise or margarine and use one of the following for moisture:

> whole, canned green chiles - cut lengthwise
> lettuce and tomato
> sweet or mild onion
> avocado slices*
> well-drained coleslaw

Alfalfa sprouts

Use in place of lettuce. They don't get soggy.

Pita bread pockets

Cut whole grain pita bread in half.
Fill with raw vegetables and tuna salad or lean sliced turkey.

* Avocado is an excellent source of fiber and a rich source of heart-healthy monosaturated fats.

Hot pita sandwich

Spray a skillet with non-stick cooking spray.
Over medium heat, cook chopped lean meat and vegetables until meat is done and vegetables are tender. Cut whole grain pita bread in half.
Fill with cooked lean meat and vegetables.

Submarine sandwich

Layer on a whole grain roll: lean meats, low-fat cheese, sliced onion and chopped lettuce. Use a nonfat or low-fat Italian dressing on the lettuce.

Cream cheese

Spread a thin layer of cream cheese (light or fat-free) on whole wheat bread or a bagel. Add slices of lean meat such as smoked turkey or roast beef and sprouts or lettuce.

Turkey special

On your favorite whole grain bread, layer: sliced turkey, cream cheese (light or fat-free), cranberry sauce and sprouts.

Deli wrap

Layer lean meat and low-fat cheese on a flavored tortilla wrap. Add some of the following: tomato slices, relishes, cranberry sauce, plain or flavored cream cheese (light or fat-free), chopped lettuce and/or sprouts. Roll up for a tasty sandwich.

Reuben sandwich

Layer on whole wheat toast: smoked turkey, rinsed and well drained sauerkraut, and part-skim mozzarella cheese. Heat under broiler until cheese is melted. Top with a slice of toast or serve open-face.

Chicken barbecue sandwich

Microwave (or cook in a skillet) a chicken breast (without bone or skin). Cook until chicken is no longer pink. Serve on a whole grain bun. Top with lettuce, a tomato slice and barbecue sauce.

Menus

Listed below are recipes from this book. They are grouped with a suggestion of what can be added to complete a meal. Refer to each recipe page for serving size and nutrient information and adjust the serving size to meet your individual needs.

Visit **www.quickandhealthy.net** for a listing of individual dinner menus.

Serve alone or add a salad.

The following recipes contain starch*, nonstarchy vegetable* and protein. Serve alone or complete the meal with a salad or raw vegetable slices.

Sandwiches and Pizza
Boboli Pizza - Sausage Style
Boboli Pizza - Shrimp Style
Meatball Sandwich
Piled High Vegetable Pizza

Meatless
Quick Lasagne
Puffy Chile Relleno Casserole

Poultry
Chicken and Artichokes Dijon
Chicken and Rice Casserole
Mediterranean Chicken
Mexican Style Chicken and Rice
Chicken Fajitas
Baked Chimichangas
Chicken and Biscuits
Chicken Enchiladas
Green Chile Chicken
    Enchilada Casserole

Beef or Pork
Fajitas Barbecue Style
Beef or Pork Fajitas
Pork and Rice Casserole

*see page 45

Seafood
Mediterranean Seafood

Ground Meat
Quick Meat and Bean Supper
Creamy Cabbage Stir-fry
John Torrey
Moore
Quick Meat Lasagne
Smoked Sausage & Rice Casserole
Spaghetti and Meatballs
Tortilla Pie

Soups
Thai Chicken Soup
Quick & Healthy Tortilla Soup
Taco Soup
Sausage and Bean Soup
Chili Con Carne

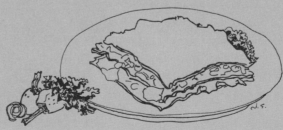

Serve alone or add a whole grain roll.

The following recipes contain starch*, nonstarchy vegetable* and protein. Serve alone or complete the meal with a whole grain roll or another whole grain product.

Chinese Chicken Salad
Oriental Rice and Seafood Salad
Sausage and
   Sauerkraut

Add a whole grain roll.

The following recipes contain nonstarchy vegetable* and protein. Serve with a whole grain roll or another whole grain product.

Curry Tuna Salad
Cinnamon Chicken Salad
Chicken and Fruit Salad
Chicken and Spinach Salad
Shrimp Salad
Italian Cioppino
Chilled Tomato-Shrimp Soup
Barbecued Smoked Sausage &
   Cabbage Casserole
Italian Zucchini Frittata
Spanish Zucchini Frittata

Add a starchy vegetable, noodles, or brown rice.

The following recipes contain nonstarchy vegetable* and protein. Serve with a starch* such as noodles, brown rice or a starchy vegetable* (corn or peas, or potatoes). Another choice is a whole grain roll or another whole grain product.

Poultry

Spicy Chicken and Grapes
Sweet and Sour Chicken
Chicken and Broccoli Casserole
Chicken Breasts Florentine
Chicken Cacciatore
Rolled Chicken and Asparagus
Teriyaki Chicken Stir-Fry
Chicken and Pea Pod Stir-fry
Chicken and Vegetables in Gravy
Mandarin Orange Chicken
Chicken in Salsa
Chicken Picadillo

Beef and Pork

Pork or Beef Stir-Fry
Chinese Pepper Steak
Italian Pork Skillet
Pork Chop Suey
Asparagus Topped
   Meatloaf

Seafood

Fish in Salsa
Spanish Baked Fish
Mandarin Orange Seafood
Spicy Seafood with Grapes

*see page 45

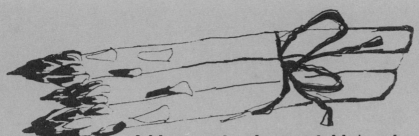

Add a nonstarchy vegetable* and a starch*.

The following recipes contain mostly protein. To balance the meal, add a nonstarchy vegetable*, either cooked or raw. Also add a starch* such as noodles, brown rice, whole grain roll or a starchy vegetable such as corn, peas or potatoes.

Poultry
Polynesian Chicken
Oven Fried Chicken
Yogurt Cumin Chicken
Chicken Breasts in Mushroom Sauce
Chicken Breasts Supreme
Chicken Nuggets
Crispy Potato Chicken
French Glazed Chicken
Hickory Smoked Barbecued Chicken
Grilled Chicken with
   Coconut-Cilantro Sauce
Grilled Chicken with Corn Salsa
Grilled Chicken with Fruit Salsa
Chicken Lettuce Wraps

Ground Meat
Pizza Meat Loaf
Meat Patties
Meat Loaf
Swedish Meatballs
Turkey Lettuce Wraps
Crustless Quiche
Beef Lettuce Wraps

Seafood
Polynesian Fish
Fillets of Sole Thermidor
Lemon Fish
Oven Fried Fish
Poached Fish
Salmon Cakes
Sweet Mustard Fish
Tarragon Fish
Yogurt Cumin Fish
French Glazed Fish
Hickory Smoked Barbecued Fish
Grilled Fish with Fruit Salsa
Grilled Salmon with
   Coconut-Cilantro Sauce
Grilled Salmon with Corn Salsa
Shrimp Lettuce Wraps

Beef and Pork
Marinated Steak
Oven Fried Pork Loin
Orange Pork Chops

*see page 45

Add a salad or raw vegetable sticks.

The following recipes contain starch* and protein. Serve with a nonstarchy vegetable* such as celery and carrot sticks or a tossed salad.

Chicken Tortilla Casserole
Clam Fettucini
Biscuits and Gravy
Crusty Calzone
Sloppy Joes
Turkey French Dips
Chicken in a Pocket
Mulligatawny Soup
New England Fish Chowder

Add a protein.

The following recipes contain nonstarchy vegetable* and starch*. To add additional protein, include a serving of a low-fat cheese, nonfat yogurt or nonfat milk. You may also want to add a raw vegetable or a roll.

Minestrone Soup
Oriental Noodle Soup
Three Bean Soup
Italian Broccoli and Pasta
Tomato and Basil Pasta

* **Starch:** breads, bagels, bulgur, couscous, noodles, rice, cereals, tortillas, dried beans; **starchy vegetables:** corn, peas, potatoes, yams, winter squash

Nonstarchy vegetables: salad greens, asparagus, artichokes, broccoli, Brussels sprouts, cabbage, carrots, cauliflower, celery, cucumbers, eggplant, green and wax beans, cooked greens, mushrooms, onions, peppers, radishes, snow peas, spinach, summer squash, tomatoes, water chestnuts, zucchini

Products Worth Trying

Listed below are some products, with a brief description, that are worth trying. Although brand names may be mentioned, there are probably other brands with similar nutrient value.

Visit www.quickandhealthy.net for more products worth trying.

Fresh Chopped or Minced Garlic - You'll find it in the produce section of the grocery store. Use 1/2 teaspoon in place of one garlic clove.

Dried Chopped Onion - This is sold in the section with seasonings and herbs. Use 2 tablespoons to replace 1/2 cup chopped raw onion.

Rice Vinegar - Rice vinegar is very good on salads. Sweeten with sugar or artificial sweetener to taste. One tablespoon is 0 calories.

Balsamic Vinegar - This very flavorful vinegar can be used on salads without the addition of other ingredients. One tablespoon is 10 calories.

Lite Soy Sauce - Most have 50% less sodium than regular soy sauce. Or you can dilute regular soy sauce with an equal amount of water to reduce the sodium. One teaspoon of the regular, diluted with an equal amount of water (total is now 2 teaspoons), is 3 calories and 306 mg of sodium (153mg of sodium for 1 teaspoon). One teaspoon of the lite version is 3 calories and 190 mg of sodium.

Butter Flavored Sprinkles - These are good sprinkled on vegetables. One half teaspoon contains 4 calories and 90 mg of sodium.

Hickory Seasoning Liquid Smoke - Just a drop adds a very good smoky flavor. Good in marinades.

Ground Fresh Chili Paste - Adds hot spiciness to Asian dishes. Available in the Asian foods section of the grocery store.

Non-stick Cooking Spray - Use for frying without adding extra calories. Or buy a spray pump and fill it will olive or canola oil. Just pump and spray.

Canola Oil - This oil contains the least amount of saturated fat and the most amount of monosaturated fat.

Olive oil - This flavorful oil is high in monosaturated fat and is a very good choice. The extra virgin has the strongest flavor and is the one I prefer.

Sesame Oil - This is another oil high in monosaturated fat. It has a distinct flavor that is very good in salads, sauces and for stir-frying.

Reduced Calorie Mayonnaise - This product may be labeled as "imitation" or "light." One tablespoon contains about 50 calories.

Nonfat Yogurts - Choose from plain, sweetened with sugar or sweetened with artificial sweetener. Calories vary from 80 to 150 for 6-8 ounces.

Fat-Free Sour Cream - There are several good brands on the market. These have a good flavor and only 10 calories for one tablespoon!

Salad Dressings - Many are available that are low in fat or are fat-free.

Quick-Cooking Brown Rice - Cooks in only 10 minutes!

Spaghetti Sauce - Look for less than 4 grams of fat for four ounces.

Cheese - Many low-fat varieties are now on the market. I prefer to buy the ones with 3-5 grams of fat per ounce. These seem to taste better than those lower in fat and they also melt more like regular cheese.

Laughing Cow Light Cheese - This spreadable cheese is available in a variety of light flavors. Each 3/4 ounce wedge contains 2 grams of fat, 35 calories, and 260 mg of sodium.

Fat-Free Feta Cheese - Surprisingly, this has a great flavor and only 30 calories for one ounce! This should be limited by those on a sodium restricted diet as it has 450 mg of sodium for 1 ounce.

Parmesan Cheese - The flavor of fresh is far better than the grated you purchase in a can. Available in the deli section of your local grocery store, either grated or whole. Inexpensive hand graters are also available.

Light Cream Cheese and Fat-Free Cream Cheese - These are a good replacement for regular cream cheese. The light contains about half the fat and about 30 calories for one tablespoon. The fat-free has only 15 calories for one tablespoon.

Egg Substitute - This product can be found in the refrigerated section of grocery store. These are a good choice for people advised to limit whole eggs. Most products are fat-free and are only 30 calories for 1/4 cup.

Fat-Free Refried Beans - An excellent source of fiber with no fat.

Low-Fat Canned Chili - Several brands are available that meet the goal of no more than 30% of the calories from fat. Check the label and look for those with no more than 8 grams of fat per 240 calories (usually 1/2 can). An excellent source of fiber.

Chicken Tenderloins - The tenderloins are the most tender part of the breast and what I prefer. Usually found in packages individually frozen.

Ground Turkey - Look for packages of lean ground turkey that have only 7% fat. Be aware that much of the ground turkey sold contains 15% fat.

Ground Beef - Choose the very lean ground beef with only 7% fat.

Smoked Turkey Sausage - This looks like and tastes like Polish kielbasa but it is much lower in fat. It is still high in sodium, so limit the amount.

Frozen T.V. Dinners - When choosing a T.V. dinner, look for those with less than 800 mg of sodium and fat providing no more than 30% of the calories. If the dinner is about 300 calories, the fat should be 10 grams or less.

Canned Soups - There are several brands that have low-fat or fat-free soups, and some that are also lower in sodium. Choose soups with less than 30% of the calories from fat.

Packaged Coleslaw Vegetables - Just add dressing. No chopping!

Alfalfa Sprouts - Great in sandwiches! These are ready to use right from the container.

Fat-Free Whipped Topping - Available in the freezer section. Only 15 calories for two tablespoons.

Fat-free Hot Cocoa Mix - Only 25 calories and 5 grams of carbohydrate per cup.

Beverages

In this section, you'll find refreshing drinks for hot summer days and an assortment of blended drinks that are great for a snack or an addition to a healthy breakfast.

Orange Julius

2 1/2 cups nonfat milk
8 ounces nonfat plain yogurt
6 ounces frozen orange
   juice concentrate
1 teaspoon vanilla extract

Process all ingredients in a
blender until smooth.

Makes 4 1/2 cups
6 servings

Each Serving
3/4 cup

Carb Servings
1 1/2

Exchanges
1 fruit
1/2 nonfat milk

Nutrient Analysis
calories 113
total fat 0g
saturated fat 0mg
cholesterol 3mg
sodium 74mg
total carbohydrate 22g
dietary fiber 0g
sugars 21g
protein 6g

Fruit Milk Shake

1/2 cup nonfat milk
1/2 cup sliced fruit (peaches, strawberries, etc.)
2 ice cubes
1/2 teaspoon vanilla extract
sweetener to taste: 1 to 2 teaspoons sugar
   or the equivalent in artificial sweetener

Process the first four ingredients in a blender until
smooth.

Sweeten to taste.

Variations:
   Yogurt Fruit Shake - Substitute nonfat yogurt for the milk.
   Buttermilk Fruit Shake - Substitute buttermilk for the milk.

Makes 1 serving

Each Serving

Carb Servings
1

Exchanges
1 fruit - 1/2 with
   artificial sweetener
1/2 nonfat milk

Nutrient Analysis
calories 96 - with
   artificial sweetener 80
total fat 0g
saturated fat 0mg
cholesterol 2mg
sodium 51mg
total carbohydrate 19g - with
   artificial sweetener 14g
dietary fiber 2g
sugars 18g - with
   artificial sweetener 14g
protein 5g

Wine Cooler

**1 cup sugar-free soda pop (Fresca, lemon
   lime, gingerale, tonic water, Sprite,
   Club Soda, seltzer water, etc.)
1/2 cup wine (white, red or blush)
ice cubes**

Fill a tall glass with ice cubes.

Add soda pop and wine. Stir to mix.

Note: Burgundy wine with Fresca combine to give a good flavor
and a berry pink color.

Makes 1 serving

Each Serving

Carb Servings
0

Exchanges
2 fat

Nutrient Analysis
calories 80
total fat 0g
saturated fat 0mg
cholesterol 0mg
sodium 41mg
total carbohydrate 1g
dietary fiber 0g
sugars 0g
protein 0g

Banana Milk Shake

**1/2 small banana (try frozen)*
1/2 cup nonfat milk
1/4 teaspoon almond extract
2 ice cubes (optional)
sweetener to taste: 1 teaspoon sugar or
   the equivalent in artificial sweetener**

Process the first four ingredients in a blender until
smooth.

Sweeten to taste.

*Cooking tip: If using frozen bananas, freeze them in the peel.
Let them sit out at room temperature about ten minutes for
easier peeling. Take advantage of bananas on sale and freeze
several to have on hand. The bananas give an ice cream texture.

Makes 1 serving

Each Serving

Carb Servings
1 1/2 - with
   artificial sweetener 1

Exchanges
1 fruit
1/2 nonfat milk

Nutrient Analysis
calories 115 - with
   artificial sweetener 99
total fat 0g
saturated fat 0mg
cholesterol 2mg
sodium 62mg
total carbohydrate 24g - with
   artificial sweetener 20g
dietary fiber 1g
sugars 18g - with
   artificial sweetener 13g
protein 5g

Makes 1 serving

Each Serving

Carb Servings
0

Exchanges
free

Nutrient Analysis
calories 15
total fat 0g
saturated fat 0mg
cholesterol 0mg
sodium 23mg
total carbohydrate 4g
dietary fiber 0g
sugars 4g
protein 0g

Cran-Raspberry Cooler

1/2 cup diet Squirt
1/2 cup light cran-raspberry juice drink
ice cubes

Fill a tall glass with ice.

Add Squirt and juice. Enjoy!

Note: Be sure to look for the light version of the juice as
it has two-thirds less calories and sugar than the regular version.

Makes 1 serving

Each Serving

Carb Servings
1

Exchanges
1 fruit

Nutrient Analysis
calories 56
total fat 0g
saturated fat 0mg
cholesterol 0mg
sodium 36mg
total carbohydrate 13g
dietary fiber 0g
sugars 10g
protein 1g

Juice Cooler

1 cup sugar-free soda pop (lemon lime,
**   Sprite, tonic water, Fresca, etc.)**
1/2 cup fruit juice, unsweetened
ice cubes

Fill a tall glass with ice cubes.

Add soda pop and juice. Stir to mix.

Cooking tip: Try this recipe with orange juice and lemon soda
or use other juices for variety. Garnish with lemon or lime slice.

Appetizers

Keep calories and fat within reasonable limits by using nonfat sour cream and nonfat yogurt in recipes. Using vegetables for dipping will add fiber and keep the calories low.

Great for a party! Serve with raw vegetables such as cucumber slices, carrot sticks and celery. This is also good when spread on small slices of whole grain bread and broiled.

Makes 3 cups
12 servings

Each Serving
1/4 cup

Carb Servings
0

Exchanges
1 vegetable
1 fat

Nutrient Analysis
calories 70
total fat 4g
saturated fat 1mg
cholesterol 6mg
sodium 182mg
total carbohydrate 4g
dietary fiber 2g
sugars 1g
protein 3g

Hot Artichoke and Spinach Dip

1/2 cup light mayonnaise
1/2 cup nonfat plain yogurt
1/2 cup grated Parmesan cheese
2 teaspoons dried or 3 tablespoons fresh
** minced onion**
1 teaspoon chopped garlic
1/2 teaspoon dried basil
1/8 teaspoon ground black pepper
1 package (10 ounces) frozen chopped spinach,
** thawed, drained and squeezed**
1 can (14 ounces) artichoke hearts, drained
** & coarsely chopped**

Preheat oven to 350 degrees.

Mix together mayonnaise, yogurt, Parmesan cheese, onion, garlic, basil and pepper.

Add spinach and artichoke hearts. Mix until blended.

Spread evenly in a pie plate that has been sprayed with non-stick cooking spray.

Bake for 25 minutes or until heated throughout.

Spinach Dip

1 package (10 ounces) frozen chopped spinach
1/4 package (2 tablespoons) dry vegetable
**   soup mix**
1 3/4 cups nonfat plain yogurt
1 can (8 ounces) water chestnuts, drained
**   and chopped**
1/4 cup light mayonnaise
2 tablespoons chopped green onion
1/4 teaspoon ground mustard

Thaw spinach, drain and squeeze until dry.

Stir dry soup before measuring to mix evenly.

Combine all ingredients and mix well.

Chill and serve with raw vegetables or slices of whole grain bread.

This is a low-calorie version of a favorite hors d'oeuvre. It looks impressive if you hollow a round loaf of whole grain bread and fill it with the dip. Cube the bread that you remove and use it to spread the dip on.

Makes 3 1/2 cups
14 servings

Each Serving
1/4 cup

Carb Servings
0

Exchanges
1 vegetable

Nutrient Analysis
calories 42
total fat 2g
saturated fat 0mg
cholesterol 2mg
sodium 84mg
total carbohydrate 5g
dietary fiber 1g
sugars 3g
protein 2g

This is a delicious spread that even children like. Liquid smoke gives a special flavor, but it can be omitted. Red canned salmon or leftover fresh salmon work the best in this recipe.

Makes about 3 cups
24 servings

Each Serving
2 tablespoons

Carb Servings
0

Exchanges
1 lean meat

Nutrient Analysis
calories 52
total fat 3g
saturated fat 2mg
cholesterol 13mg
sodium 138mg
total carbohydrate 2g
dietary fiber 0g
sugars 1g
protein 5g

Smoked Salmon Spread

1 tub (12 ounces) light cream cheese
1/2 cup nonfat sour cream
1 tablespoon lemon juice
1 1/2 teaspoons Worcestershire sauce
1 teaspoon liquid smoke
1/8 teaspoon salt (optional)
1/8 teaspoon ground black pepper
1 can (14 ounces) red salmon, drained or 2 cups
**   cooked and flaked fresh salmon**
2 tablespoons chopped celery
2 tablespoons chopped green onion

Have cream cheese at room temperature.

Blend the first seven ingredients in a mixer.

Remove skin from salmon and mash bones, if using canned.

Mix salmon, celery and onion with the cream cheese mixture.

Spread on raw vegetables or whole grain crackers.

Chinese Barbecued Pork

1 pound boneless pork tenderloin (2 inches wide)
1/2 cup Chinese barbecue sauce
2 tablespoons ground mustard or bottled hot
  mustard

Marinate pork in barbecue sauce overnight (or at least 4 hours) in refrigerator. Discard marinade.

Preheat oven to 325 degrees.

Roast meat for 1 hour or until meat juices run clear.

Slice 1/8 inch thick and serve hot or refrigerate and serve cold.

To make hot mustard sauce from ground mustard: Mix 2 tablespoons of ground mustard with an equal amount of cold water.

Stir until the consistency of thick cream.

Allow to sit 10 minutes to develop full flavor.

To serve: Dip pork in hot mustard sauce.

This is as good as the barbecued pork you order as an appetizer in Chinese restaurants. You can also serve this as a main dish.

Makes 16 servings

Each Serving
1 ounce pork

Carb Servings
0

Exchanges
1 lean meat

Nutrient Analysis
calories 47
total fat 2g
saturated fat 0mg
cholesterol 16mg
sodium 42mg
total carbohydrate 2g
dietary fiber 0g
sugars 1g
protein 7g

Mock Sour Cream

1 cup low-fat cottage cheese
1/4 cup nonfat milk

Place all ingredients in blender.

Process on high speed until smooth and creamy.

Use on baked potatoes or as a vegetable dip.

Variation: *Dill Sour Cream Dip* – Add 1 teaspoon of dried dill weed to mixture when blending.

Creamy Seafood Dip

4 ounces light cream cheese
2 cups low-fat cottage cheese
3 tablespoons lemon juice
2 teaspoons prepared horseradish
1/4 teaspoon Tabasco sauce
1/4 cup chopped green onion
1 can (6 ounces) minced clams, shrimp,
**   or crab, drained**

Have cream cheese at room temperature.

In a blender or food processor, mix cheeses with the next three ingredients until smooth.

Stir in onions and seafood. Serve with raw vegetables or whole grain crackers.

Variation: *Smoky Seafood Dip* - Add 1 teaspoon of hickory flavor liquid smoke when blending ingredients.

Breads

Using oat bran or oats, and replacing

part of the white flour with whole wheat flour,

adds fiber to breads. The texture becomes somewhat coarser

but very acceptable. All of the breads in this section use less

sugar than what is typical in sweetened breads.

Makes 12 muffins

Each Serving
1 muffin

Carb Servings
1

Exchanges
1 starch
1 fat

Nutrient Analysis
calories 121
total fat 4g
saturated fat 0mg
cholesterol 0mg
sodium 140mg
total carbohydrate 20g
dietary fiber 3g
sugars 9g
protein 4g

Oat Bran Muffins

2 1/4 cups oat bran
1/4 cup firmly packed brown sugar
1 tablespoon baking powder
1 1/2 teaspoons ground cinnamon
3/4 cup nonfat milk
1/4 cup egg substitute (equal to 1 egg)
2 tablespoons oil (canola)
1 cup unsweetened applesauce
1 banana, mashed
2 tablespoons dried fruit such as raisins,
   dates, apricots (optional)

Preheat oven to 425 degrees.

Mix the first four ingredients in a large bowl. Set aside.

Combine milk, egg and oil. Mix applesauce with mashed banana and blend with liquid ingredients. Add to dry ingredients and mix just until moistened.

Pour into muffin tins that have been sprayed with non-stick cooking spray. Do not use paper liners as the muffins have a tendency to stick to the paper.

Bake for 15-17 minutes.

Note: One serving is a good source of fiber.

Refrigerator Bran Muffins

2 cups All Bran Cereal
2 cups boiling water
4 cups buttermilk
2 1/2 cups sugar
1 cup egg substitute (equal to 4 eggs)
1 cup oil (canola)
3 cups whole wheat flour
2 cups unbleached all-purpose flour
5 teaspoons baking soda
1 1/4 teaspoons salt (optional)
2 cups dried fruit (optional)
4 cups Bran Buds or 100% Bran cereal

In a small bowl, pour boiling water over the All Bran cereal and let stand until softened.

In a large bowl, mix buttermilk, sugar, eggs and oil. Add the All Bran/water mixture to the egg mixture.

Mix the flours, baking soda and salt in a small bowl. Stir into the egg mixture and mix just until moistened. If using dried fruit, add now. Stir in Bran Buds or 100% Bran cereal.

Follow directions below for microwave or conventional oven.

Conventional Oven: Preheat oven to 375 degrees. Pour about 1/4 cup batter into muffin tins sprayed with non-stick cooking spray or tins lined with cupcake papers. Bake for 15 minutes (20 minutes for chilled batter).

Microwave Oven: For one muffin: Pour 1/4 cup batter into cupcake paper. Cook on high 55-70 seconds, rotating 1/4 turn halfway through cooking.

Note: One serving is a good source of fiber.

Make this recipe to have on hand for fresh baked breakfast muffins. The batter can be covered and stored in the refrigerator for up to three weeks and baked as needed. These are lower in sugar and fat than most bran muffins.

Makes 56 muffins

Each Serving
1 muffin

Carb Servings
1 1/2

Exchanges
1 1/2 starch
1/2 fat

Nutrient Analysis
calories 142
total fat 5g
saturated fat 0mg
cholesterol 1mg
sodium 188mg
total carbohydrate 25g
dietary fiber 4g
sugars 12g
protein 3g

Applesauce adds moistness and flavor to this coffee cake. Make this large amount and freeze half for another breakfast. This is lower in sugar and fat than most coffee cakes.

Makes 24 servings

Each Serving

Carb Servings
1 1/2

Exchanges
1 1/2 starch
1/2 fat

Nutrient Analysis
calories 153
total fat 4g
saturated fat 0mg
cholesterol 0mg
sodium 136mg
total carbohydrate 25g
dietary fiber 2g
sugars 9g
protein 4g

Applesauce Oatmeal Coffee Cake

3 cups oats (quick or old fashioned)
1 1/2 cups unbleached all-purpose flour
1 cup whole wheat flour
1 cup firmly packed brown sugar
2 teaspoons baking powder
1 1/2 teaspoons baking soda
1 teaspoon ground allspice
1/2 teaspoon ground cinnamon
2 cups unsweetened applesauce
1 cup nonfat milk
6 tablespoons oil (canola)
1/2 cup egg substitute (equal to 2 eggs)
optional topping: 2 tablespoons firmly
    packed brown sugar and 1/4 teaspoon
    ground cinnamon

Preheat oven to 375 degrees.

Combine the first eight ingredients in a large bowl.

Mix the next four ingredients in a small bowl. Add to the dry ingredients and stir just until moistened.

Pour into a 9-inch by 13-inch baking dish that has been sprayed with non-stick cooking spray. Sprinkle optional topping ingredients over batter.

Bake for 35-40 minutes or until golden brown.

Variations: Make half of this recipe and bake in a 9-inch by 9-inch baking pan for 25-30 minutes.
Applesauce Oatmeal Muffins - For muffins, bake at 400 degrees for 15-20 minutes. The full recipe makes about 24 muffins.

Blueberry Coffee Cake

2 cups oats (quick or old fashioned)
1 2/3 cups unbleached all-purpose flour
1 cup whole wheat flour
1 cup firmly packed brown sugar
1 tablespoon baking powder
1 teaspoon salt (optional)
1 teaspoon ground cinnamon
1/2 teaspoon ground cloves
2 cups nonfat milk
1/2 cup egg substitute (equal to 2 eggs)
6 tablespoons oil (canola)
2 cups fresh or frozen blueberries
optional topping: 2 tablespoons firmly
packed brown sugar and 1/4 teaspoon
ground cinnamon

Preheat oven to 375 degrees.

Combine the first eight
ingredients in a large bowl.

Mix milk, egg and oil in a small bowl.
Add to the dry ingredients and mix just until
moistened. Add blueberries.

Pour into a 9-inch by 13-inch baking pan that
has been sprayed with non-stick cooking spray.

Bake for 35-40 minutes or until golden brown.

Variations: Make half of this recipe and bake in a 9-inch by
9-inch baking pan for 25-30 minutes.
Blueberry Muffins - For muffins, bake at 425 degrees for 15-20
minutes. The full recipe makes about 24 muffins.

---

*This large coffee cake
is great for a brunch.
It also freezes well. See
the variations below for
a smaller coffee cake or
for making muffins.
This is lower in sugar
and fat than most
coffee cakes.*

Makes 24 servings

Each Serving

Carb Servings
1 1/2

Exchanges
1 1/2 starch
1/2 fat

Nutrient Analysis
calories 146
total fat 4g
saturated fat 0mg
cholesterol 0mg
sodium 82mg
total carbohydrate 24g
dietary fiber 2g
sugars 8g
protein 4g

Makes 12 servings

Each Serving

Carb Servings
1

Exchanges
1 starch

Nutrient Analysis
calories 104
total fat 1g
saturated fat 0mg
cholesterol 0mg
sodium 215mg
total carbohydrate 20g
dietary fiber 1g
sugars 1g
protein 3g

Italian Focaccia Bread

1 loaf (1 pound) whole wheat Focaccia bread
1 teaspoon olive oil
1 teaspoon Italian seasoning
1 teaspoon grated Parmesan cheese

Preheat oven to 375 degrees.

Spread olive oil over top of bread.

Sprinkle with Italian seasoning and cheese.

Bake for 20 minutes or until golden brown.

Dumplings

1/2 cup whole wheat flour
1/2 cup unbleached all-purpose flour
1 teaspoon baking powder
1/8 teaspoon salt (optional)
1/3 cup nonfat milk
1/4 cup egg substitute (equal to 1 egg)

Combine dry ingredients.

Mix milk and egg substitute. Blend with dry ingredients, just until moistened.

Drop by spoonfuls onto simmering liquid. Follow directions below for microwave or stovetop.

Microwave Oven: Cover and cook on high for 7 minutes, rotating 1/4 turn halfway through cooking time.

Stovetop: Cook, uncovered, for 10 minutes. Cover and cook an additional 10 minutes.

Add a special touch to soups and stews with this simple recipe. These are good with the Chicken Cacciatore recipe in this book.

Makes 6 dumplings

Each Serving
1 dumpling

Carb Servings
1

Exchanges
1 starch

Nutrient Analysis
calories 85
total fat 0g
saturated fat 0mg
cholesterol 0mg
sodium 106mg
total carbohydrate 17g
dietary fiber 2g
sugars 0g
protein 4g

Try these for a quick supper with turkey sausage and the Fruit Sauce recipe in this book.

Makes 6 Servings
12 four-inch pancakes

Each Serving
2 pancakes

Carb Servings
1 1/2 - with
   artificial sweetener 1

Exchanges
1 1/2 starch - 1 with
   artificial sweetener
1 very lean meat

Nutrient Analysis
calories 135 - with
   artificial sweetener 119
total fat 1g
saturated fat 0mg
cholesterol 2mg
sodium 215mg
total carbohydrate 22g - with
   artificial sweetener 17g
dietary fiber 3g
sugars 6g
protein 11g

Cottage Cheese Pancakes

1 cup low-fat cottage cheese
3/4 cup egg substitute (equal to 3 eggs)
1/4 cup nonfat milk
1/4 teaspoon salt (optional)
1 cup whole wheat flour
2 tablespoons sugar or the equivalent in
   artificial sweetener

Combine the first four ingredients in blender.

Process until smooth. Add flour and sugar and blend again.

Spray a griddle with non-stick cooking spray. When hot, pour batter onto griddle to make 12 pancakes.

Cook until golden brown on both sides.

Note: One serving is a good source of fiber.

Gravies and Sauces

You'll find a few sauces in this section that will add interest to meals and satisfy your palate. Also included are fat-free gravies that taste great without the extra calories.

Spanish Yogurt Sauce

1 cup nonfat plain yogurt
1/2 cup salsa, thick and chunky
1 teaspoon dried parsley
1/2 teaspoon dried cilantro (optional)
1/4 teaspoon ground cumin

Mix all ingredients and refrigerate until serving.

Serving tip: This goes well with Mexican food, over baked fish or over sliced tomatoes and cucumbers.

Makes 1 1/2 cups
6 servings

Each Serving
1/4 cup

Carb Servings
0

Exchanges
1 vegetable

Nutrient Analysis
calories 27
total fat 0g
saturated fat 0mg
cholesterol 1mg
sodium 129mg
total carbohydrate 4g
dietary fiber 0g
sugars 4g
protein 2g

Thick and Chunky Salsa

1 can (14 ounces) diced tomatoes*
2 medium tomatoes, chopped (about 2 cups)
6 green onions, chopped
1/2 cup chopped fresh cilantro
1 can (4 ounces) diced green chiles
1 tablespoon chopped garlic
1/2 teaspoon salt (optional)
1/8 teaspoon ground black pepper

Combine all ingredients.

Serve with your favorite Mexican food or as a dip.

*Sodium is figured for reduced-salt.

Note: Choose mild to hot chiles to suit your taste.

Makes 4 cups
16 servings

Each Serving
1/4 cup

Carb Servings
0

Exchanges
free

Nutrient Analysis
calories 14
total fat 0g
saturated fat 0mg
cholesterol 0mg
sodium 28mg
total carbohydrate 3g
dietary fiber 1g
sugars 2g
protein 1g

Fresh Cucumber
Sauce for Seafood

1 cup chopped cucumber, not peeled
1/2 cup nonfat plain yogurt
1/4 cup chopped green onion
1/4 cup light mayonnaise
1 tablespoon lemon juice
1 teaspoon Dijon mustard
1 teaspoon dried minced onion or
   1 tablespoon fresh minced onion
1/4 teaspoon salt (optional)

Combine all ingredients.

Cover and chill before serving.

Serve cold with seafood.

Serve this with the Oven Fried Fish or the Oven Fried Oysters recipe in this book. It's a good low-fat replacement for tartar sauce.

Makes 2 cups
8 servings

_____

Each Serving
1/4 cup

Carb Servings
0

Exchanges
1/2 vegetable
1/2 fat

Nutrient Analysis
calories 37
total fat 3g
saturated fat 1mg
cholesterol 3mg
sodium 87mg
total carbohydrate 3g
dietary fiber 0g
sugars 1g
protein 1g

Makes 1 1/4 cups
5 servings

Each Serving
1/4 cup

Carb Servings
1/2 - with
  artificial sweetener 0

Exchanges
1/2 fruit
free with
  artificial sweetener

Nutrient Analysis
calories 32 - with
  artificial sweetener 19
total fat 0g
saturated fat 0mg
cholesterol 0mg
sodium 1mg
total carbohydrate 8g - with
  artificial sweetener 4g
dietary fiber 3g
sugars 5g - with
  artificial sweetener 2g
protein 0g

Fruit Sauce

**1 1/2 cups fresh raspberries or sliced strawberries
or one 12-ounce package frozen raspberries
or strawberries
4 teaspoons sugar or the equivalent in
artificial sweetener
1 tablespoon lemon juice**

Fresh fruit: Place 1/2 cup of fruit in a blender with sweetener and lemon juice. Blend until smooth. Add remaining fruit and stir into mixture.

Frozen fruit: Thaw fruit. Place half of the fruit in blender with sweetener and lemon juice. Blend until smooth. Drain remaining fruit and stir into mixture.

Note: One serving is a good source of fiber.

Flour Gravy

1 cup fat-free cold broth,* divided (chicken, turkey or beef)
2 tablespoons unbleached all-purpose flour
seasonings to taste

Pour 1/4 cup of broth in a covered container. Add flour and shake well to prevent lumps.

Follow directions below for microwave or stovetop.

Stovetop: In a small saucepan, combine remainder of broth with flour mixture. Cook on medium until boiling, while stirring constantly with a wire whisk. Continue stirring until thickened.

Microwave Oven: In a 4-cup glass measuring cup, combine remainder of broth with flour mixture. Heat on high for 2-3 minutes (stirring well with a wire whisk after each minute) or until thickened.

*Sodium is figured for reduced-salt.

Note: Use 3 1/2 tablespoons of flour for one 14-ounce can of broth.

Variation: *Mushroom Gravy* - Add one small can of drained mushrooms after the gravy is thickened.

This will remind you of traditional gravy but it is so much lower in calories because it has no fat. You can use canned broth or instant bouillon mixed with water.

Makes 1 cup
8 servings

Each Serving
2 tablespoons

Carb Servings
0

Exchanges
free

Nutrient Analysis
calories 9
total fat 0g
saturated fat 0mg
cholesterol 0mg
sodium 47mg
total carbohydrate 2g
dietary fiber 0g
sugars 0g
protein 1g

Cornstarch Gravy

1 cup cold fat-free broth,* divided (chicken, turkey or beef)
1 tablespoon cornstarch
seasonings to taste

Pour 1/4 cup broth in a small container. Add cornstarch and mix well.

Follow directions below for microwave or stovetop.

Stovetop: In a small saucepan, combine remainder of broth with cornstarch mixture. Cook on medium until boiling, while stirring constantly with a wire whisk. Continue stirring until thickened.

Microwave Oven: In a 4-cup glass measuring cup, combine remainder of broth with cornstarch mixture. Heat on high for 2-3 minutes (stirring well with a wire whisk after each minute) or until thickened.

*Sodium is figured for reduced-salt.

Note: Use 1 3/4 tablespoons cornstarch for one 14-ounce can of broth.

Variation: *Mushroom Gravy* - Add one small can of drained mushrooms after the gravy is thickened.
For a thicker gravy, increase cornstarch to 1 1/2 tablespoons.

This gravy contains no fat. It is the consistency of sauces used in Chinese food and has a clearer appearance than a flour gravy. Canned broth works well in this recipe.

Makes 1 cup
8 servings

Each Serving
2 tablespoons

Carb Servings
0

Exchanges
free

Nutrient Analysis
calories 6
total fat 0g
saturated fat 0mg
cholesterol 0mg
sodium 47mg
total carbohydrate 1g
dietary fiber 0g
sugars 0g
protein 0g

Soups and Stews

Soups are great for a cold winter day. Several of these recipes make a large amount, so plan on leftovers or freeze for later use. Freezing in one-cup containers makes a perfect choice for lunch. Many of these recipes are high in fiber.

Makes 8 cups
5 servings

Each Serving
1 1/2 cups

Carb Servings
1

Exchanges
3 vegetable
1/2 fat

Nutrient Analysis
calories 91
total fat 3g
saturated fat 0mg
cholesterol 0mg
sodium 22mg
total carbohydrate 16g
dietary fiber 3g
sugars 10g
protein 3g

Gazpacho

1 large cucumber, not peeled, quartered
2 medium tomatoes, quartered
1 green bell pepper, quartered
1 medium onion, quartered
3 cups tomato juice,* divided
1 tablespoon olive oil
1 tablespoon lemon juice
1 teaspoon chopped garlic
1/2 teaspoon hot pepper sauce (optional)
1/4 teaspoon salt (optional)
1/4 teaspoon ground black pepper
dash cayenne pepper

Optional Toppings
1/2 – 1 cup chopped fresh cilantro
nonfat sour cream or nonfat plain yogurt

In a blender or food processor, combine the cucumber, tomato, green pepper, onion and 1 1/2 cups of the tomato juice.

Process the ingredients until mixture is still chunky.

Mix in remaining ingredients. Chill thoroughly.

Serve in small bowls topped with cilantro and sour cream or yogurt.

*Sodium is figured for reduced-salt.

Note: One serving is a good source of fiber.

Zero Vegetable Soup

1 can (14 ounces) fat-free broth* (chicken or beef)
1 1/2 cups sliced vegetables, any combination of:
    cabbage, broccoli, carrots, onions, zucchini, celery
    tomatoes, cauliflower, mushrooms

Follow directions below for microwave or stovetop.

Stovetop: Mix all ingredients in a small saucepan. Cover and simmer for 10-15 minutes or until vegetables are tender.

Microwave Oven: Mix all ingredients in a 1-quart glass bowl. Cover and cook on high for about 5-10 minutes (stir twice during cooking) until vegetables are tender.

*Sodium is figured for reduced-salt.

Makes 2 1/2 cups
2 servings

Each Serving
1 1/4 cups

Carb Servings
1/2

Exchanges
1 vegetable

Nutrient Analysis
calories 35
total fat 0g
saturated fat 0mg
cholesterol 0mg
sodium 335mg
total carbohydrate 6g
dietary fiber 2g
sugars 3g
protein 3g

Chilled Tomato-Shrimp Soup

1 cup tomato juice*
1/2 cup cooked and cleaned shrimp
1/2 tablespoon lemon juice
1/2 teaspoon prepared horseradish
1/8 teaspoon Worcestershire sauce
1 drop Tabasco sauce

Combine all ingredients. Chill before serving.

*Sodium is figured for reduced-salt.

Makes 1 1/2 cups
1 serving

Each Serving

Carb Servings
1

Exchanges
2 vegetable
2 very lean meat

Nutrient Analysis
calories 129
total fat 1g
saturated fat 0mg
cholesterol 166mg
sodium 235mg
total carbohydrate 11g
dietary fiber 1g
sugars 9g
protein 20g

I like the flavor of this seafood stew. Don't limit yourself to just fish since shrimp, clams and crab also taste good in this dish.

Makes 6 cups
4 servings

Each Serving
1 1/2 cups

Carb Servings
1 1/2

Exchanges
4 vegetable
3 very lean meat

Nutrient Analysis
calories 207
total fat 2g
saturated fat 0mg
cholesterol 43mg
sodium 169mg
total carbohydrate 22g
dietary fiber 4g
sugars 13g
protein 27g

Italian Cioppino

1 can (28 ounces) diced tomatoes,* not drained
1 can (8 ounces) tomato sauce*
1 cup chopped onion
1/2 cup fat-free chicken broth* or white wine
1 tablespoon dried parsley
2 teaspoons chopped garlic
1 teaspoon each: dried basil, dried thyme, dried
marjoram and dried oregano
1 bay leaf
1/4 teaspoon ground black pepper
1 pound fish fillets (or shrimp, clams, crab)

Add all ingredients, except fish, in a medium saucepan.

Simmer for 20 to 30 minutes, stirring occasionally.

Meanwhile, cut fish into 1/2 inch chunks. Add fish to saucepan and cook 10 minutes or until done.

Discard bay leaf before serving.

*Sodium is figured for reduced-salt.

Note: One serving is a good source of fiber.

Cooking tip: Use a combination of seafood such as shrimp, clams, and crab. If uncooked, add with the fish. If using precooked seafood, just add to heat.

Variation: *Italian Cioppino with Zucchini* - Add 2 cups sliced zucchini before simmering.

 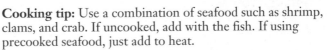

New England Fish Chowder

1 1/2 cups diced new potatoes
1 cup water
1/2 cup chopped green pepper
1/2 cup chopped onion
1/2 teaspoon dried thyme
2 cups nonfat milk
2 tablespoons cornstarch
1/2 teaspoon salt (optional)
1/8 teaspoon ground black pepper
3/4 pound fish fillets, cut into 1-inch pieces
1/4 pound scallops (fish can be substituted)

In a medium saucepan, combine the first five ingredients and bring to a boil.

Reduce heat to low and simmer, covered, for 15 minutes or until potatoes are tender.

Mix cornstarch with milk and remaining seasonings. Stir into soup and bring to a boil, stirring constantly until slightly thickened.

Reduce heat and add seafood.

Simmer until seafood is cooked.

This low-calorie version of chowder has an excellent flavor.

Makes 6 cups
4 servings

Each Serving
1 1/2 cups

Carb Servings
1 1/2

Exchanges
1 starch
1/2 nonfat milk
3 very lean meat

Nutrient Analysis
calories 220
total fat 2g
saturated fat 0mg
cholesterol 43mg
sodium 156mg
total carbohydrate 22g
dietary fiber 2g
sugars 8g
protein 28g

The light coconut milk adds a unique Thai flavor without the extra fat and sugar that is in regular coconut milk. If you like spicy foods, add the larger amount of fresh chili paste.

Makes 9 cups
6 servings

Each Serving
1 1/2 cups

Carb Servings
1 1/2

Exchanges
1 starch
1 vegetable
2 1/2 very lean meat

Nutrient Analysis
calories 227
total fat 5g
saturated fat 4mg
cholesterol 43mg
sodium 324mg
total carbohydrate 21g
dietary fiber 3g
sugars 4g
protein 23g

Thai Chicken Soup

1 pound skinless, boneless chicken breasts, cut into bite-size pieces
2 cups fat-free chicken broth*
2 cups water
1 can (13 ounces) light coconut milk
2 cups bite-size broccoli pieces
2 cups snow pea pods, cut in half
1 red bell pepper, cut into bite-size pieces (about 1 cup)
4 ounces angel hair pasta, broken into small pieces
1 tablespoon minced fresh ginger
1 tablespoon chopped garlic
1 tablespoon lite soy sauce
1/2 - 1 tablespoon ground fresh chili paste
1 teaspoon ground cumin
1/2 cup chopped fresh cilantro (optional)

In a large saucepan that has been sprayed with non-stick cooking spray, sauté chicken for a few minutes.

Add remaining ingredients, except cilantro. Bring to a boil.

Reduce heat to low. Cover and simmer for 10-15 minutes or until noodles are cooked and vegetables are tender.

Serve topped with fresh cilantro.

*Sodium is figured for reduced-salt.

Note: One serving is a good source of fiber.
Fresh chili paste can be found in the Asian foods section of your grocery store.

Oriental Noodle Soup

5 cups fat-free chicken broth*
3/4 teaspoon garlic powder
1/4 teaspoon ground black pepper
3 ounces angel hair pasta
4 green onions, sliced thin
3/4 cup thinly sliced mushrooms
1/2 cup thinly sliced carrots

Combine the first three ingredients in a medium stockpot. Bring to a boil.

Break pasta into small pieces.

Add pasta and vegetables to the stockpot. Cook for 5-6 minutes or until pasta is tender.

*Sodium is figured for reduced-salt.

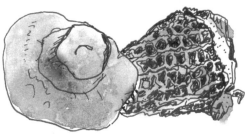

This is a light soup with a good flavor. I especially like the fineness of the angel hair pasta in this recipe.

Makes 6 cups
6 servings

Each Serving
1 cup

Carb Servings
1

Exchanges
2/3 starch
1 vegetable

Nutrient Analysis
calories 79
total fat 1g
saturated fat 0mg
cholesterol 0mg
sodium 326mg
total carbohydrate 14g
dietary fiber 1g
sugars 2g
protein 5g

French Onion Soup

6 cups fat-free beef broth*
1 1/2 cups thinly sliced onions
1/4 teaspoon ground black pepper
6 slices whole grain or French bread, toasted
3/4 cup (3 ounces) grated, reduced-fat
 mozzarella cheese

Mix the first three ingredients in a medium saucepan and simmer for 20 minutes.

Divide soup into 6 ovenproof bowls. Top each with a slice of toasted bread and 1/2 ounce of cheese. Broil until cheese is melted.

*Sodium is figured for reduced-salt.

Taco Soup

1 pound extra lean ground beef or ground
 turkey (7% fat)
1 medium onion, chopped
2 cans (15 ounces each) pinto or
 chili beans, not drained
1 can (15 ounces) tomato sauce*
2 cans (14 ounces each) diced tomatoes,*
 not drained
1/2 package taco seasoning

Brown meat with onion in a stockpot that has been sprayed with non-stick cooking spray.

Add remaining ingredients and simmer for 30 minutes.

*Sodium is figured for reduced-salt.

Note: One serving is an excellent source of fiber.

Mulligatawny Soup

1 pound skinless, boneless chicken breasts,
   cut into bite-size pieces
4 cups fat-free chicken broth*
2/3 cup quick-cooking brown rice
1 medium apple, peeled and diced
   (about 1 1/2 cups)
1/2 cup chopped onion
1 1/2 teaspoons curry powder
1/2 teaspoon salt (optional)
1/4 teaspoon ground black pepper
3 tablespoons unbleached
   all-purpose flour
1 cup water

In a large saucepan, sauté chicken for three minutes.

Add chicken broth, rice, apple, onion, curry, salt and pepper. Bring to a boil.

Reduce heat to low. Cover and simmer for 10 minutes.

Meanwhile, in a covered container, combine water and flour. Shake well to prevent lumps.

Stir into hot soup. Bring to a boil, stirring constantly for one minute or until slightly thickened.

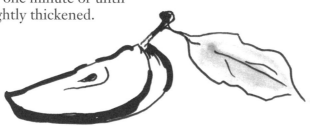

*Sodium is figured for reduced-salt.

The ingredients may seem a bit unusual but they combine to make a wonderfully unique flavor. This is a simple meal that you can complete with a salad. Add more curry if you like spicy foods.

Makes 8 cups
4 servings

Each Serving
2 cups

Carb Servings
1 1/2

Exchanges
1 starch
1/2 fruit
4 very lean meat

Nutrient Analysis
calories 248
total fat 2g
saturated fat 0mg
cholesterol 65mg
sodium 456mg
total carbohydrate 24g
dietary fiber 2g
sugars 6g
protein 31g

Makes 2 1/2 quarts
10 servings

Each Serving
1 cup

Carb Servings*
1

Exchanges*
3/4 starch
1 vegetable

Nutrient Analysis
calories 110
total fat 1g
saturated fat 0mg
cholesterol 1mg
sodium 180mg
total carbohydrate 20g
dietary fiber 5g
sugars 4g
protein 6g

*reflects carbohydrate
 minus fiber

Minestrone Soup

**1/3 cup each: dried green split peas, dried
   lentils and pearl barley**
1/2 cup dried black-eyed peas
4 1/2 cups water
3 1/2 cups fat-free beef broth*
**2 1/2 cups chopped vegetables of your choice:
   celery, onion, zucchini, carrots,
   green pepper, mushrooms, etc.**
1 can (14 ounces) diced tomatoes,* not drained
2 teaspoons dried basil
1 1/2 teaspoons dried oregano
1 teaspoon salt (optional)
1 teaspoon chopped garlic
1/2 teaspoon ground black pepper
2 bay leaves
3 tablespoons grated Parmesan cheese

Wash peas, lentils and barley. Mix with water and broth in a large kettle.

Bring to a boil. Reduce heat, cover and simmer for 30 minutes.

Add remaining ingredients and simmer another hour or until peas are tender. Discard bay leaves.

Serve sprinkled with Parmesan cheese.

*Sodium is figured for reduced-salt.

Note: One serving is an excellent source of fiber.

Three Bean Soup

3 cups water
1 can (28 ounces) diced tomatoes,* not drained
1 can (15 ounces) kidney beans, drained
1 can (15 ounces) black eyed peas, drained
1 can (15 ounces) garbanzo beans, drained
1 can (6 ounces) tomato paste*
1 tablespoon Dijon mustard
1 1/2 teaspoons chopped garlic
1 teaspoon chili powder
1 teaspoon dried basil
1 teaspoon dried oregano
1/2 teaspoon ground cumin
1/2 teaspoon ground black pepper
1 can (15 ounces) whole kernel corn,* drained
1 cup chopped carrots
1 cup chopped zucchini or celery
1 medium onion, chopped

Combine the first thirteen ingredients in a large stockpot.

Bring to a boil.

Reduce heat and simmer, covered, for 10 minutes.

Stir in remaining vegetables and simmer, covered, for an additional 10 minutes.

*Sodium is figured for reduced-salt.

Note: One serving is an excellent source of fiber.

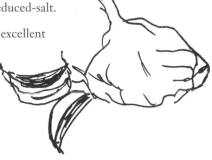

This can be cooked in less than 30 minutes since almost every ingredient is canned. You can omit the fresh vegetables or substitute any vegetable of your choice.

Makes 3 quarts
12 servings

Each Serving
1 cup

Carb Servings*
1

Exchanges*
1 starch
1 vegetable

Nutrient Analysis
calories 126
total fat 1g
saturated fat 0mg
cholesterol 0mg
sodium 129mg
total carbohydrate 26g
dietary fiber 8g
sugars 7g
protein 7g

*reflects carbohydrate minus fiber

This is a meal in a bowl and the best part is that it can be prepared in minutes. This makes a large amount so plan on leftovers. We especially like the spicy flavor and the fresh cilantro.

Makes 12 cups
8 servings

Each Serving
1 1/2 cups

Carb Servings*
2

Exchanges*
1 1/3 starch
1 vegetable
2 lean meat

Nutrient Analysis
calories 261
total fat 6g
saturated fat 2mg
cholesterol 35mg
sodium 877mg
total carbohydrate 38g
dietary fiber 12g
sugars 8g
protein 19g

***reflects carbohydrate
  minus fiber**

Sausage and Bean Soup

**1 package (16 ounces) low-fat turkey
    smoked sausage**
1 medium onion chopped
**4 cans (about 15 ounces each) of beans
    of your choosing, all drained
    Beans that work well are: black, kidney,
    pinto, garbanzo, lima**
1 can (14 ounces) diced tomatoes,* not drained
2 cups fat-free chicken broth*
2 cups water
1 can (4 ounces) diced green chiles
1/2 cup salsa, thick and chunky
1 cup chopped fresh cilantro

Cut sausage into bite-size pieces.

In a large kettle, combine all ingredients except the cilantro. Bring to a boil.

Reduce heat to low. Cover and simmer for 10 minutes.

Serve topped with cilantro.

*Sodium is figured for reduced-salt.

Note: One serving is an excellent source of fiber.
This recipe is higher in sodium and should be limited by those on a low-sodium diet.

Chili Con Carne

**2 pounds extra lean ground beef or ground
     turkey (7% fat)**
3 cans (15 ounces each) kidney beans, drained
1 can (28 ounces) diced tomatoes,* not drained
1 can (15 ounces) tomato sauce*
2 large onions, chopped
2 medium green peppers, chopped
2 tablespoons chili powder
1/4 teaspoon paprika
2 bay leaves

Brown the ground meat in a large kettle that has been
sprayed with non-stick cooking spray.

Add remaining ingredients.

Cover and simmer for 1 hour.

Discard bay leaves
before serving.

*Sodium is figured for reduced-salt.

Note: One serving is an excellent source of fiber.

*This is a great dish for
a party because it really
makes a large amount
and it tastes so good.
I also recommend
freezing leftovers in
one-cup containers to
have handy for lunch.*

Makes 3 quarts
12 servings

Each Serving
1 cup

Carb Servings*
1

Exchanges*
1/2 starch
2 vegetable
2 lean meat

Nutrient Analysis
calories 242
total fat 6g
saturated fat 2mg
cholesterol 47mg
sodium 141mg
total carbohydrate 27g
dietary fiber 11g
sugars 7g
protein 22g

*reflects carbohydrate
 minus fiber

This flavorful soup can be prepared in minutes. It will be enjoyed by all ages.

Makes 8 cups
4 servings

Each Serving
2 cups

Carb Servings*
2

Exchanges*
2 starch
1 vegetable
2 very lean meat

Nutrient Analysis
calories 248
total fat 3g
saturated fat 0mg
cholesterol 32mg
sodium 585mg
total carbohydrate 40g
dietary fiber 7g
sugars 8g
protein 24g

*reflects carbohydrate
 minus fiber

Quick and Healthy Tortilla Soup

**1/2 pound skinless, boneless chicken breasts,
   cut into bite-size pieces
3 1/2 cups fat-free chicken broth*
1 can (15 ounces) black beans, drained and rinsed
1 can (15 ounces) whole kernel corn,* drained
1 can (14 ounces) diced tomatoes,* not drained
1 can (4 ounces) diced green chiles
3 corn tortillas (6-inch), cut in eighths**

In a medium saucepan, sauté chicken for three minutes.

Add broth, beans, corn, tomatoes and chiles. Simmer for 10 minutes.

Add tortillas and simmer for an additional 10 minutes.

*Sodium is figured for reduced-salt.

Note: One serving is an excellent source of fiber.

Vegetables

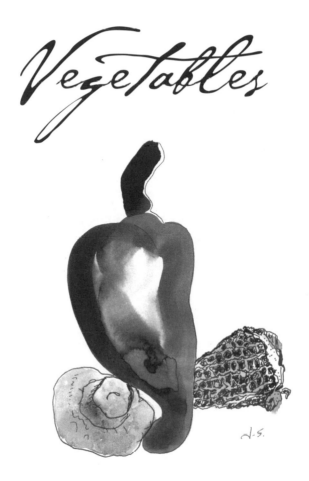

Recipes in this section include hot and cold vegetable dishes that work well with almost any meal. When preparing fresh vegetables, cook in the microwave or steam just until crisp-tender.

Baked Portobello Mushrooms

4 portobello mushrooms
1 teaspoon olive oil
1/4 teaspoon dried rosemary
1/8 teaspoon salt (optional)
dash ground black pepper

Preheat oven to 350 degrees.

Using a teaspoon, gently remove the gills (black underside). Cut off stems and discard.

Place mushrooms, top side up, on a baking sheet that has been sprayed with non-stick cooking spray.

Brush with olive oil. Sprinkle with rosemary, salt and pepper.

Bake for 10 minutes.

Roasted Eggplant Medley

**1 small eggplant, not peeled (about 12-14 ounces),
cut into one-inch cubes (about 4 cups)**
1 onion, cut in eighths
1 cup chopped bell pepper, green or yellow
1 tablespoon chopped garlic
1 teaspoon Italian seasoning
1/2 teaspoon salt (optional)
1/4 teaspoon ground black pepper
2 medium tomatoes, chopped (about 2 cups)

Preheat oven to 400 degrees.

In a large bowl, mix vegetables, except tomatoes, with garlic and seasonings.

Spread in a 9-inch by 13-inch baking pan that has been sprayed with non-stick cooking spray.

Roast for 10-15 minutes.

Add tomatoes and return to oven for 5 minutes or until all vegetables are tender.

Note: One serving is a good source of fiber.

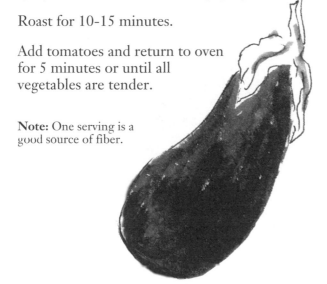

This is an attractive side dish that goes well with beef, fish or chicken.

Makes 4 cups
8 servings

Each Serving
1/2 cup

Carb Servings
1/2

Exchanges
1 vegetable

Nutrient Analysis
calories 30
total fat 0g
saturated fat 0mg
cholesterol 0mg
sodium 4mg
total carbohydrate 7g
dietary fiber 3g
sugars 3g
protein 1g

Zucchini, Tomato and Onion

2 cups sliced onion
2 cups sliced tomato
2 cups sliced zucchini
1 1/2 teaspoons Italian seasoning
1/2 teaspoon salt (optional)
dash of ground black pepper

Preheat oven to 350 degrees.

Layer onion, tomato, and zucchini in a 2-quart casserole dish that has been sprayed with non-stick cooking spray.

Sprinkle each layer with seasonings.

Bake for 30-45 minutes, or until vegetables are tender.

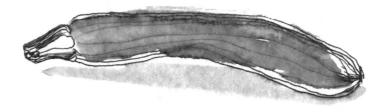

Makes 3 1/2 cups
7 servings

Each Serving
1/2 cup

Carb Servings
1/2

Exchanges
1 vegetable

Nutrient Analysis
calories 29
total fat 0g
saturated fat 0mg
cholesterol 0mg
sodium 7mg
total carbohydrate 7g
dietary fiber 2g
sugars 3g
protein 1g

Basil Tomatoes

2 medium tomatoes, diced or sliced (about 2 cups)
1 teaspoon dried basil
1 teaspoon chopped garlic
1/2 teaspoon salt (optional)
1/8 teaspoon ground black pepper

Mix ingredients and let sit at room temperature for at least one hour.

Serve plain or on a lettuce leaf.

Note: The addition of basil gives an excellent flavor to fresh tomatoes.

Makes 2 cups
4 servings

Each Serving
1/2 cup

Carb Servings
0

Exchanges
free

Nutrient Analysis
calories 18
total fat 0g
saturated fat 0mg
cholesterol 0mg
sodium 5mg
total carbohydrate 4g
dietary fiber 1g
sugars 2g
protein 1g

Italian Tomatoes

2 cups sliced tomatoes
1/4 cup red wine vinegar
1/4 teaspoon Italian seasoning
1/8 teaspoon ground black pepper
1/8 teaspoon garlic powder

Arrange tomatoes in a shallow bowl.

Mix remaining ingredients and pour over tomatoes.

Marinate 1/2 hour, at room temperature, before serving.

Makes 2 cups
4 servings

Each Serving
1/2 cup

Carb Servings
0

Exchanges
free

Nutrient Analysis
calories 19
total fat 0g
saturated fat 0mg
cholesterol 0mg
sodium 5mg
total carbohydrate 5g
dietary fiber 1g
sugars 3g
protein 1g

Gourmet Cucumbers

1/3 cup rice vinegar
1 tablespoon sugar or the equivalent
   in artificial sweetener
1 medium cucumber, not peeled, thinly sliced
   (about 2 cups)
1 cup sliced sweet onion
1/4 teaspoon ground black pepper
1/4 teaspoon dried dill weed (optional)

Mix vinegar with sugar. Add remaining ingredients.

Serve immediately or marinate in the refrigerator for
2 or 3 hours.

Serve with a slotted spoon or drain liquid before
serving.

Marinated Vegetables

4 cups water
4 cups vegetables, cut into bite-size pieces, such
   as: broccoli, celery, green pepper, carrots,
   mushrooms, cauliflower, green beans
1/4 cup reduced-fat Italian dressing

Bring water to a boil. Add vegetables and return to a boil.
Drain immediately.

Mix vegetables with Italian dressing and marinate in the
refrigerator for one hour or until well chilled. Drain
before serving.

Salsa Vegetables

1 cup chopped cucumber, not peeled,
1 can (14 ounces) diced tomatoes* or
   1 1/2 cups chopped fresh tomato
1 can (8 ounces) whole kernel corn,* drained
1/2 cup chopped bell pepper, red or green
1/4 cup chopped fresh cilantro
2 tablespoons red wine vinegar
1/2 teaspoon garlic powder
1/2 teaspoon ground cumin
1/4 teaspoon salt (optional)
1/8 teaspoon ground black pepper
1/8 teaspoon cayenne pepper

Combine ingredients and mix well.

Serve cold.

*Sodium is figured for reduced-salt.

Serve this as a cold side dish with Mexican food. It is colorful and has a great flavor.

Makes 4 cups
8 servings

Each Serving
1/2 cup

Carb Servings
1/2

Exchanges
1 vegetable

Nutrient Analysis
calories 30
total fat 0g
saturated fat 0mg
cholesterol 0mg
sodium 13mg
total carbohydrate 7g
dietary fiber 1g
sugars 4g
protein 1g

This dish can be served either hot or cold. The rice vinegar and bacon bits add a good flavor to the beans.

Makes 4 servings

Each Serving

Carb Servings
1/2 - with
   artificial sweetener 0

Exchanges
1 vegetable

Nutrient Analysis
calories 28 - with
   artificial sweetener 26
total fat 0g
saturated fat 0mg
cholesterol 0mg
sodium 21mg
total carbohydrate 6g - with
   artificial sweetener 5g
dietary fiber 2g
sugars 2g - with
   artificial sweetener 1g
protein 1g

Seasoned Green Beans

1 tablespoon water
1 tablespoon dried or 1/4 cup fresh
   minced onion
1 can (14 ounces) green beans,* drained
1 tablespoon rice vinegar
2 teaspoons bacon-flavored soy bits
1/2 teaspoon sugar or the equivalent in
   artificial sweetener
1/4 teaspoon ground black pepper

Mix the first two ingredients in a medium bowl.

Let sit for 5-10 minutes.

Add remaining ingredients and mix well.

Serve hot or cold.

*Sodium is figured for reduced-salt.

Salads

Salad making can
be quick if you buy
pre-washed and cut vegetables.
Using a food processor also saves time, especially if you
chop foods for several recipes at once. Salads in this section
include main dishes, side dishes and salads that can be served
on a bed of lettuce or used as a sandwich spread.

Tangy grapefruit and mild avocado add variety to salad greens and make this a delicious and enjoyable salad.

Grapefruit and Avocado Salad

1 avocado
2 tablespoons lime juice
1 grapefruit, peeled
1/2 cup thinly sliced green onions
10-12 ounces mixed salad greens
   (about 2 quarts), torn

Dressing:
2 tablespoons apple cider vinegar
1 tablespoon olive oil
1 tablespoon water
2 teaspoons sugar, or the equivalent in
   artificial sweetener
1/4 teaspoon ground cumin
1/8 teaspoon ground black pepper
1/8 teaspoon salt (optional)

Peel and slice the avocado. Pour lime juice over avocado to prevent browning.

Section grapefruit and cut into bite-size pieces.

In a large salad bowl, mix grapefruit, green onion and salad greens.

Drain avocado, reserving lime juice. Mix reserved lime juice with dressing ingredients.

Add avocado to the salad. Pour dressing over salad and toss.

Note: One serving is an excellent source of fiber.
Most of the fat in this recipe is heart-healthy monosaturated fat.

Makes 10 cups
5 servings

Each Serving
2 cups

Carb Servings*
1 - with
   artificial sweetener 1/2

Exchanges*
1/2 fruit
1 vegetable - 1/2 with
   artificial sweetener
1 1/2 fat

Nutrient Analysis
calories 134 - with
   artificial sweetener 128
total fat 8g
saturated fat 1mg
cholesterol 0mg
sodium 30mg
total carbohydrate 16g - with
   artificial sweetener 14g
dietary fiber 5g
sugars 10g - with
   artificial sweetener 8g
protein 3g

***reflects carbohydrate
 minus fiber**

Pear Salad with Raspberry Dressing

2 pears, chopped, not peeled (about 3 cups)
1 tablespoon lemon juice
10-12 ounces mixed salad greens
(about 2 quarts), torn
1/2 cup chopped walnuts or almonds
1/2 cup reduced-fat raspberry salad dressing

In a large salad bowl, mix chopped pears with lemon juice to prevent browning.

Add salad greens and nuts.

Pour dressing over salad and toss.

Note: One serving is an excellent source of fiber. Most of the fat in this recipe is polyunsaturated fat.

Variation: *Apple Salad with Raspberry Dressing* - Substitute chopped apples for the pears.

Makes 10 cups
5 servings

Each Serving
2 cups

Carb Servings*
1

Exchanges*
1 fruit
1 vegetable
2 fat

Nutrient Analysis
calories 196
total fat 11g
saturated fat 1mg
cholesterol 0mg
sodium 243mg
total carbohydrate 24g
dietary fiber 5g
sugars 15g
protein 3g

***reflects carbohydrate
 minus fiber**

This is a refreshing salad that goes well with many dishes.

Apple Salad Mold

1 small box (0.3 ounces) sugar-free cherry-flavored gelatin*
1 cup boiling water
1/2 cup apple juice
1/2 cup cold water
1 medium apple, not peeled, chopped (about 1 1/2 cups)
1/2 cup chopped celery

Dissolve gelatin in boiling water.

Combine juice and cold water. Add to gelatin and stir well.

Refrigerate until slightly thickened.

Add apple and celery. Mix well.

Refrigerate until set.

*Any flavor of gelatin can be substituted.

Makes 2 1/2 cups
5 servings

Each Serving
1/2 cup

Carb Servings
1/2

Exchanges
1/2 fruit

Nutrient Analysis
calories 39
total fat 0g
saturated fat 0mg
cholesterol 0mg
sodium 51mg
total carbohydrate 8g
dietary fiber 1g
sugars 6g
protein 1g

Fruit Salad

4 cups sliced fruit
1 cup fruit flavored nonfat yogurt
(sweetened with artificial
sweetener)

Mix fruit with yogurt in a
serving bowl.

You can make this recipe
different each time by varying
the fruit and the flavor of yogurt.

Makes 4 cups
8 servings

Each Serving
1/2 cup

Carb Servings
1

Exchanges
1 starch

Nutrient Analysis
calories 60
total fat 0g
saturated fat 0mg
cholesterol 1mg
sodium 23mg
total carbohydrate 14g
dietary fiber 1g
sugars 10g
protein 2g

Lime Cottage Salad

1 small box (0.3 ounces) sugar-free, lime
flavored gelatin
1 cup nonfat plain yogurt
2 cups low-fat, small curd cottage cheese
1 can (20 ounces) crushed pineapple
(packed in juice), drained
2 cups nonfat whipped topping

Mix gelatin with yogurt in a medium bowl.
Add cottage cheese and pineapple. Mix well.

Gently mix in whipped topping.

This is ready to serve or can be refrigerated
for later use.

Makes 5 1/2 cups
7 servings

Each Serving
3/4 cup

Carb Servings
1

Exchanges
1/2 fruit
1/2 nonfat milk
1 very lean meat

Nutrient Analysis
calories 121
total fat 1g
saturated fat 0mg
cholesterol 3mg
sodium 328mg
total carbohydrate 16g
dietary fiber 0g
sugars 10g
protein 11g

The sweet, tangy dressing makes this salad a stand out. Also, the sesame oil adds a unique flavor to this salad. The almonds can be toasted days ahead.

Makes 10 cups
5 servings

Each Serving
2 cups

Carb Servings*
1

Exchanges*
1 fruit - 2/3 with
 artificial sweetener
1 high-fat meat
3 fat

Nutrient Analysis
calories 286 - with
 artificial sweetener 272
total fat 22g
saturated fat 3mg
cholesterol 0mg
sodium 118mg
total carbohydrate 22g - with
 artificial sweetener 19g
dietary fiber 8g
sugars 12g - with
 artificial sweetener 8g
protein 6g

***reflects carbohydrate
 minus fiber**

Romaine and Mandarin Orange Salad

1/2 cup slivered almonds, toasted
2 avocados
1 tablespoon lime juice
10-12 ounces romaine lettuce (about 2 quarts), torn
2 cans (11 ounces each) mandarin oranges, drained

Dressing:
1/3 cup rice vinegar
2 tablespoons sesame oil
**1 1/2 tablespoons sugar or
   the equivalent in artificial
   sweetener**
2 teaspoons lite soy sauce
2 teaspoons water
1/2 teaspoon ground ginger
1/2 teaspoon ground mustard
1/2 teaspoon salt (optional)
1/2 teaspoon ground black pepper

Toasted almonds: Preheat oven to 400 degrees. Place almonds on a baking sheet that has been sprayed with non-stick cooking spray. Bake for 3 minutes. Stir and return to oven for an additional 2 minutes. Set on a wire rack to cool.

Salad: Peel and slice avocados. In a large salad bowl, pour lime juice over avocado to prevent browning. Add lettuce and mandarin oranges.

Mix dressing ingredients and shake well. Pour over salad ingredients and toss. Top with toasted almonds.

Note: One serving is an excellent source of fiber.
Although this recipe is high in overall fat, most of it is heart-healthy monosaturated fat.

Romaine Salad with Berries and Maple Nuts

1 cup walnut halves
1/4 cup sugar-free or regular maple syrup
10-12 ounces romaine lettuce (about 2 quarts), torn
2 cups fresh berries, such as blueberries or
    raspberries

Dressing:
3 tablespoons red wine vinegar
3 tablespoons water
2 tablespoons canola or olive oil
2 teaspoons Dijon mustard
1 teaspoon dried or 1 tablespoon
    fresh minced onion
1/2 teaspoon chopped garlic
1/4 teaspoon salt (optional)
1/4 teaspoon ground black pepper

Walnuts: Preheat oven to 400 degrees. In a small bowl, stir together walnuts and maple syrup to coat. Spread walnuts on a baking sheet that has been sprayed with non-stick cooking spray. Bake for 3 minutes. Stir and return to oven for an additional 2 minutes. Set on a wire rack to cool.

Salad: Meanwhile, mix the dressing ingredients and shake well.

In a large salad bowl, add lettuce, walnuts and berries. Toss with dressing.

Note: One serving is a good source of fiber.
Although this recipe is high in overall fat, most of it is polyunsaturated fat.

Variation: *Romaine Salad with Fruit and Maple Nuts* - Substitute seedless grapes, sliced apples or sliced pears for the berries.

This flavorful salad is popular with all ages. The walnuts can be prepared ahead of time and you can also save time by toasting a larger quantity and storing them for future use.

Makes 10 cups
5 servings

Each Serving
2 cups

Carb Servings
1

Exchanges
2/3 fruit
1 vegetable
3 1/2 fat

Nutrient Analysis
calories 222
total fat 17g
saturated fat 2mg
cholesterol 0mg
sodium 94mg
total carbohydrate 17g
dietary fiber 4g
sugars 8g
protein 4g

Makes 3 cups
4 servings

Each Serving
3/4 cup

Carb Servings
1/2

Exchanges
1 vegetable
2 fat

Nutrient Analysis
calories 119
total fat 10g
saturated fat 1mg
cholesterol 0mg
sodium 8mg
total carbohydrate 8g
dietary fiber 4g
sugars 2g
protein 2g

Mexican Garden Salad

1 medium tomato, sliced and quartered
 (about 1 cup)
1 cup sliced cucumber, not peeled
1 cup chopped sweet onion
1 avocado, peeled and sliced
1/2 cup chopped fresh cilantro
1 tablespoon lime juice
1 tablespoon olive oil
1/4 teaspoon ground cumin
1/4 teaspoon salt (optional)
1/8 teaspoon ground black pepper

In a medium bowl, mix vegetables with remaining ingredients. Serve as is or on a bed of lettuce.

Note: One serving is a good source of fiber.
Most of the fat in this recipe is heart-healthy monosaturated fat.

Italian Garden Salad

1 medium tomato, sliced and quartered
  (about 1 cup)
1 cup sliced cucumber, not peeled
1 cup chopped sweet onion
1 tablespoon olive oil
1 1/2 teaspoons dried basil
1 1/2 teaspoons chopped garlic
1/2 teaspoon salt (optional)
1/8 teaspoon ground black pepper

Combine all ingredients. Let sit out for thirty minutes
to one hour, at room temperature, before serving.
Serve alone or on a lettuce leaf.

Makes 3 cups
4 servings

Each Serving
3/4 cup

Carb Servings
3/4

Exchanges
1 vegetable
1 fat

Nutrient Analysis
calories 58
total fat 4g
saturated fat 0mg
cholesterol 0mg
sodium 6mg
total carbohydrate 6g
dietary fiber 1g
sugars 2g
protein 1g

Greek Salad

1 green pepper, sliced
1 red pepper, sliced
1 yellow pepper, sliced
1 cucumber, not peeled, sliced
3 tablespoons red wine vinegar
2 tablespoons lemon juice
1/4 teaspoon dried oregano
4 ounces nonfat feta cheese

Mix peppers and cucumber in a large bowl.

Add vinegar, lemon juice and oregano. Mix well.

Cover and marinate for 15 minutes to several hours.

Toss well before serving and top with crumbled
feta cheese.

Makes 8 cups
8 servings

Each Serving
1 cup

Carb Servings
0

Exchanges
1 vegetable
1/2 very lean meat

Nutrient Analysis
calories 33
total fat 0g
saturated fat 0mg
cholesterol 0mg
sodium 227mg
total carbohydrate 5g
dietary fiber 1g
sugars 3g
protein 4g

Broccoli Salad

4 cups broccoli florets
2 tomatoes, chopped
1 cup sliced mushrooms
4 teaspoons bacon-flavor soy bits

Dressing:
1/4 cup light mayonnaise
1 tablespoon dried parsley
1/4 teaspoon onion powder
1/8 teaspoon garlic powder

Mix vegetables and bacon bits in a medium bowl.

Make dressing by combining seasonings with mayonnaise.

Add dressing to vegetables and mix well.

Note: One serving is a good source of fiber.

This makes a large amount so it is a good choice for a potluck. If you prefer the crunch of the soy bacon bits, add them just before serving.

Makes 6 cups
6 servings

Each Serving
1 cup

Carb Servings
1/2

Exchanges
1 vegetable
1 fat

Nutrient Analysis
calories 68
total fat 4g
saturated fat 1mg
cholesterol 3mg
sodium 124mg
total carbohydrate 6g
dietary fiber 3g
sugars 3g
protein 3g

Three Bean Salad

1/4 cup rice vinegar
1 tablespoon sugar or the equivalent in
** artificial sweetener**
1 tablespoon dried or 1/4 cup fresh minced onion
1 can (14 ounces) green beans,* drained
1 can (8 ounces) garbanzo beans, drained
1 can (8 ounces) kidney beans, drained
1 tablespoon dried parsley
1/4 teaspoon onion powder
1/8 teaspoon garlic powder

In a medium bowl, combine vinegar, sugar and onion.

Let sit for 5 minutes.

Add beans and seasonings. Mix well.

Drain before serving.

*Sodium is figured for reduced-salt.

Note: One serving is an excellent source of fiber.

Keep these canned beans on hand so you can put together a salad in just a few minutes.

Makes 3 cups
6 servings

Each Serving
1/2 cup

Carb Servings*
1/2

Exchanges*
1/2 starch
1/2 vegetable

Nutrient Analysis
calories 70 - with
   artificial sweetener 62
total fat 1g
saturated fat 0mg
cholesterol 0mg
sodium 40mg
total carbohydrate 15g - with
   artificial sweetener 13g
dietary fiber 6g
sugars 4g - with
   artificial sweetener 2g
protein 4g

***reflects carbohydrate
 minus fiber**

To save time, use a food processor for chopping the cabbage. This is simple to prepare and has a good flavor.

Cabbage Salad

6 cups chopped cabbage
3 green onions, chopped
3 tablespoons toasted sesame seeds

Dressing:
3 tablespoons rice vinegar
1 tablespoon sugar or the equivalent in artificial sweetener

Mix the first three ingredients in a large bowl.

Combine rice vinegar with sugar.

Add to cabbage and toss well.

This is ready to serve or you can refrigerate it for several hours before serving.

Note: One serving is a good source of fiber.

Variations:
   Cabbage and Chicken Salad - Just before serving, add 2 cups of cooked chicken.
   Cabbage and Shrimp Salad - Just before serving, add 2 cups of cooked and cleaned shrimp. Frozen shrimp that has been thawed is preferred over canned.

Makes 6 cups
6 servings

Each Serving
1 cup

Carb Servings
1/2

Exchanges
2 vegetable

Nutrient Analysis
calories 52 - with
   artificial sweetener 44
total fat 2g
saturated fat 0mg
cholesterol 0mg
sodium 18mg
total carbohydrate 9g - with
   artificial sweetener 7g
dietary fiber 3g
sugars 6g - with
   artificial sweetener 3g
protein 2g

Vegetable Bean Salad

1/4 cup rice vinegar
1 tablespoon sugar or the equivalent in
    artificial sweetener
1 tablespoon dried or 1/4 cup fresh minced onion
1 can (8 ounces) green beans* or garbanzo
    beans, drained
1 can (8 ounces) kidney beans, drained
1 cup bite-size pieces of cauliflower or broccoli
1/2 cup sliced carrots
1 tablespoon dried parsley
1/4 teaspoon onion powder
1/8 teaspoon garlic powder

In a medium bowl, combine vinegar, sugar and onion.

Let sit for 5 minutes.

Add vegetables and seasonings. Mix well.

Drain before serving.

*Sodium is figured for reduced-salt.

Note: One serving is a good source of fiber.

This variation of the three bean salad uses fresh vegetables in place of some of the beans.

Makes 3 cups
6 servings

Each Serving
1/2 cup

Carb Servings
1 - with
    artificial sweetener 1/2

Exchanges
1/3 starch
1 vegetable

Nutrient Analysis
calories 52 - with
    artificial sweetener 44
total fat 0g
saturated fat 0mg
cholesterol 0mg
sodium 28mg
total carbohydrate 11g - with
    artificial sweetener 9g
dietary fiber 4g
sugars 4g - with
    artificial sweetener 2g
protein 3g

Makes 8 cups
10 servings

Each Serving
3/4 cup

Carb Servings
1 1/2 - with
    artificial sweetener 1

Exchanges
1 starch
1 vegetable
1 fat

Nutrient Analysis
calories 141 - with
    artificial sweetener 134
total fat 5g
saturated fat 1mg
cholesterol 4mg
sodium 152mg
total carbohydrate 21g - with
    artificial sweetener 19g
dietary fiber 2g
sugars 4g - with
    artificial sweetener 2g
protein 4g

Macaroni Salad

8 ounces uncooked elbow macaroni
2 cups sliced celery
2 cups chopped red pepper
1/2 cup chopped green onion (optional)

Dressing:
1/2 cup light mayonnaise
1/3 cup rice vinegar
1 1/2 tablespoons sugar or the equivalent
    in artificial sweetener
1 tablespoon Dijon mustard
1/4 teaspoon ground black pepper

Cook macaroni according to package directions.

Drain and cool.

Prepare vegetables and place in a large bowl.

In a small bowl, mix dressing ingredients.

Add cooled macaroni and dressing to vegetables.

Toss well.

Herb Potato Salad

**1 pound thin-skinned new potatoes, not peeled
    (about 4 cups, cubed)**
1/2 cup sliced radishes (optional)
1/2 cup sliced green onion

Dressing:
3 tablespoons nonfat plain yogurt
1 tablespoon light mayonnaise
1 1/2 teaspoons Dijon mustard
1/2 teaspoon chopped garlic
1/2 teaspoon dried basil
1/4 teaspoon dried thyme
1/4 teaspoon onion powder
1/4 teaspoon salt (optional)

Cut potatoes in 1-inch cubes.

Place in medium saucepan and cover with water.

Bring to a boil. Cover, reduce heat and simmer 12 minutes or until potatoes are tender. Drain.

Mix dressing ingredients.

Combine hot potatoes, radishes, green onion and dressing.

Serve hot or refrigerate and serve cold.

The mustard and seasonings make this a tasty potato salad. Try using new red potatoes or Yukon gold.

Makes 6 servings

Each Serving

Carb Servings
1

Exchanges
1 starch

Nutrient Analysis
calories 72
total fat 1g
saturated fat 0mg
cholesterol 1mg
sodium 65mg
total carbohydrate 14g
dietary fiber 2g
sugars 2g
protein 2g

This is a great summer meal. The combination of fruit with spinach and chicken is really good. Substitute fresh fruit of your choice.

Makes 14 cups
5 servings

Each Serving
2 3/4 cups

Carb Servings
1

Exchanges
1 fruit
2 1/2 lean meat

Nutrient Analysis
calories 190
total fat 7g
saturated fat 1mg
cholesterol 43mg
sodium 65mg
total carbohydrate 16g
dietary fiber 4g
sugars 11g
protein 19g

Chicken and Spinach Salad

Dressing:
3 tablespoons red wine vinegar
3 tablespoons orange juice
1 1/2 tablespoons canola oil
1/2 teaspoon poppy seeds
1/4 teaspoon ground mustard

6 ounces fresh spinach leaves
2 oranges, peeled and cut into chunks
2 cups small strawberries
2 cups cooked and cubed chicken

Mix dressing ingredients and set aside.

Tear spinach into bite-size pieces.

Place in a large bowl with oranges, strawberries and chicken.

Add dressing and toss well.

Note: One serving is a good source of fiber.

Chicken and Fruit Salad

Dressing:
1/3 cup nonfat strawberry yogurt (sweetened with artificial sweetener)
1 tablespoon light mayonnaise
1 tablespoon orange juice

2 cups cooked and cubed chicken or turkey
2 oranges, peeled and cut into chunks
1 cup seedless grapes
1 cup strawberries, halved
1/2 cup sliced celery
lettuce leaves

Make dressing by mixing the first three ingredients.

Combine remaining ingredients (except lettuce) in a medium bowl.

Add dressing and toss.

Serve on lettuce leaves.

Note: One serving is a good source of fiber.

Makes 7 1/2 cups
5 servings

Each Serving
1 1/2 cups

Carb Servings
1

Exchanges
1 fruit
1 vegetable
2 1/2 very lean meat

Nutrient Analysis
calories 171
total fat 3g
saturated fat 1mg
cholesterol 44mg
sodium 82mg
total carbohydrate 19g
dietary fiber 3g
sugars 15g
protein 18g

Cinnamon Chicken Salad

Dressing:
2 tablespoons light mayonnaise
2 tablespoons nonfat plain yogurt
1/2 teaspoon ground cinnamon
1/8 teaspoon ground cloves
1/8 teaspoon ground black pepper
1/8 teaspoon salt (optional)

2 cups cooked and cubed chicken or turkey
1 cup seedless grapes
1/2 cup sliced celery
8 large lettuce leaves

Mix the dressing ingredients and set aside.

Combine chicken, grapes and celery in a medium bowl.

Add dressing and toss.

Serve on lettuce leaves.

Makes 4 cups
4 servings

Each Serving
1 cup

Carb Servings
1/2

Exchanges
1/2 fruit
1 vegetable
3 very lean meat

Nutrient Analysis
calories 169
total fat 5g
saturated fat 1mg
cholesterol 57mg
sodium 125mg
total carbohydrate 10g
dietary fiber 1g
sugars 7g
protein 21g

Chinese Chicken Salad

1 small head (1 1/2 pounds) Chinese cabbage
    (Napa), shredded
2 cups cooked brown rice
2 cups cooked chicken, shredded
1 cup diagonally sliced celery
1/2 cup sliced green onion
1 can (16 ounces) bean sprouts, drained
1 can (8 ounces) sliced water chestnuts,
    drained and chopped

Soy Dressing:
2 tablespoons canola oil
1/3 cup water
2-4 tablespoons lite soy sauce*
1 tablespoon cider vinegar
1 tablespoon catsup
1 tablespoon brown sugar or the equivalent in
    artificial sweetener
1/2 teaspoon ground ginger or 2 teaspoons
    fresh grated
1/4 teaspoon chopped garlic

In a large bowl, combine the first seven ingredients.

Prepare dressing by mixing all ingredients in a covered
container and shake to blend.

Toss dressing with salad up to 4 hours or just
before serving.

For an attractive presentation, save a few of the cabbage
leaves to line a serving bowl.

*Use the lesser amount of soy sauce if on a sodium restricted diet.

Note: One serving is a good source of fiber.

This makes a large amount and is great for a potluck or a luncheon. Use a food processor to save time chopping. Save more time by using quick-cooking brown rice.

Makes 14 cups
7 servings

Each Serving
2 cups

Carb Servings
1 1/2

Exchanges
1 starch
2 vegetable
1 lean meat
1/2 fat

Nutrient Analysis
calories 210 - with
    artificial sweetener 205
total fat 6g
saturated fat 1mg
cholesterol 31mg
sodium 256mg
total carbohydrate 24g - with
    artificial sweetener 22g
dietary fiber 3g
sugars 5g - with
    artificial sweetener 4g
protein 15g

This is a delicious recipe that makes enough for a crowd. I really like the flavor you get from the soy sauce and rice vinegar. Use quick-cooking brown rice to save time.

Oriental Rice and Seafood Salad

2 cups cooked brown rice, cooled
1 pound cooked and cleaned salad shrimp
1 can (16 ounces) bean sprouts, drained
2 stalks celery, diagonally sliced
1/2 cup chopped green pepper
2 green onions, thinly sliced
1 can (8 ounces) sliced water chestnuts, drained
1/4 cup rice vinegar
2 tablespoons lite soy sauce
1 tablespoon sugar or the equivalent in artificial sweetener

Combine the first seven ingredients in a large bowl.

Mix vinegar, soy sauce and sugar.

Pour over salad and mix well.

Chill before serving.

Note: One serving is a good source of fiber.

Variation: *Oriental Rice and Chicken Salad -* Substitute 2 cups of cooked and cubed chicken for the shrimp.

Curry Tuna Salad

1 teaspoon dried or 1 tablespoon fresh
   minced onion
1 tablespoon lemon juice
2 cans (6 ounces each) water pack tuna, drained
1 can (8 ounces) sliced water chestnuts, drained
1/4 cup light mayonnaise
2 teaspoons lite soy sauce
1 teaspoon curry powder
lettuce leaves

Mix onion with lemon juice and let sit for 5 minutes.

Combine tuna and water chestnuts in a small bowl.

Make dressing by mixing mayonnaise, onion, lemon juice, soy sauce and curry.

Combine dressing with tuna and water chestnuts.

Serve on a bed of lettuce.

Variation: *Toasted Tuna Sandwich* - Spread 1/2 cup of tuna salad on half of a toasted whole grain English muffin. Heat under broiler until hot.

Try this for a different tuna salad. The taste of curry and the crunch of water chestnuts make this especially good.

Makes 3 cups
4 servings

Each Serving
3/4 cup

Carb Servings
0

Exchanges
1 vegetable
3 very lean meat
1/2 fat

Nutrient Analysis
calories 155
total fat 6g
saturated fat 1mg
cholesterol 36mg
sodium 473mg
total carbohydrate 5g
dietary fiber 1g
sugars 1g
protein 19g

Try this colorful coleslaw. It's low in fat because nonfat yogurt is used for part of the dressing. Fresh or imitation crab can be substituted for the shrimp.

Makes 8 cups
8 servings

Each Serving
1 cup

Carb Servings
1/2

Exchanges
2 vegetable
1 very lean meat

Nutrient Analysis
calories 86 - with
   artificial sweetener 80
total fat 1g
saturated fat 0mg
cholesterol 76mg
sodium 140mg
total carbohydrate 10g - with
   artificial sweetener 8g
dietary fiber 2g
sugars 7g - with
   artificial sweetener 5g
protein 11g

Shrimp Coleslaw

1 small head of cabbage, shredded (about 5 cups)
1 medium green pepper, diced
1 carrot, chopped
2 green onions, chopped
2 cups cooked and cleaned shrimp

Dressing:
1 cup nonfat plain yogurt
3 tablespoons rice vinegar
1 tablespoon sugar or the equivalent in artificial sweetener
2 teaspoons dried dill weed
1/2 teaspoon ground black pepper
1/2 teaspoon celery seed
1/2 teaspoon Dijon mustard

In a large bowl, combine vegetables with shrimp.

Mix dressing ingredients and pour over vegetables.

Serve immediately or chill for one hour before serving.

Shrimp Salad

3/4 cup rice vinegar
2 tablespoons sugar or the equivalent in
**   artificial sweetener**
1 avocado, peeled and sliced
1/2 cup chopped green onion
1/4 cup chopped fresh cilantro
1/4 teaspoon crushed red pepper
1/4 teaspoon garlic powder
10-12 ounces salad greens (about 2 quarts)
1 pound cooked and cleaned salad shrimp
1/2 cup coarsely chopped dry roasted peanuts

In a medium bowl, mix sugar with rice vinegar and stir to dissolve.

Add the next five ingredients and mix well.

Just before serving, mix salad greens with the shrimp and dressing in a large serving bowl.

Top with peanuts.

Note: One serving is an excellent source of fiber.
Most of the fat in this recipe is heart-healthy monosaturated fat.

This is a great main dish salad for a warm day. Serve with a whole grain roll to complete the meal.

Makes 12 cups
5 servings

_____

Each Serving
2 1/2 cups

Carb Servings*
1/2 - with
    artificial sweetener 0

Exchanges*
2 vegetable - 1 with
    artificial sweetener
3 very lean meat
2 fat

Nutrient Analysis
calories 247 - with
    artificial sweetener 228
total fat 12g
saturated fat 2mg
cholesterol 175mg
sodium 230mg
total carbohydrate 14g - with
    artificial sweetener 9g
dietary fiber 5g
sugars 7g - with
    artificial sweetener 2g
protein 24g

***reflects carbohydrate
 minus fiber**

This recipe is good on lettuce or as a sandwich spread. Substituting shrimp for part, or all, of the crab also tastes good. Sodium can be reduced by using fresh crab instead of the imitation.

Makes 4 cups
8 servings

Each Serving
1/2 cup

Carb Servings
1/2

Exchanges
1 vegetable
1 lean meat

Nutrient Analysis
calories 85
total fat 3g
saturated fat 1mg
cholesterol 15mg
sodium 544mg
total carbohydrate 7g
dietary fiber 0g
sugars 1g
protein 8g

Seafood Salad

1 pound imitation or fresh crab
1 cup chopped celery
1/4 cup chopped green onion
2 tablespoons light mayonnaise
2 tablespoons nonfat plain yogurt
1 tablespoon lemon juice
1/4 teaspoon paprika
1/4 cup (1 ounce) grated, reduced-fat
**   cheddar cheese**

Combine the first three ingredients in a medium bowl.

In a small bowl, combine mayonnaise, yogurt, lemon juice, and paprika. Stir in cheese.

Add to crab and mix well.

Variation: *Toasted Seafood Salad Sandwich* - Spread 1/2 cup on a toasted whole grain English muffin half and broil until cheese is melted.

Rice, Beans and Potatoes

Brown rice, potatoes with the skin, and beans all add fiber to your diet. Using quick-cooking brown rice reduces cooking time by as much as 30 minutes.

This is a colorful side dish that you can vary by using different root vegetables such as parsnips, turnips and sweet potatoes.

Makes 4 cups
4 servings

Each Serving
1 cup

Carb Servings
1 1/2

Exchanges
1 starch
1 vegetable
1/2 fat

Nutrient Analysis
calories 131
total fat 4g
saturated fat 1mg
cholesterol 0mg
sodium 51mg
total carbohydrate 23g
dietary fiber 4g
sugars 5g
protein 2g

Roasted Root Vegetables

4 small thin-skinned new potatoes, not peeled
 (about 3/4 pound)
2 cups whole baby carrots
1 onion, cut in eighths
1 tablespoon chopped garlic
1 tablespoon olive oil
1/4 teaspoon dried thyme
1/4 teaspoon dried rosemary
1/4 teaspoon ground black pepper
1/4 teaspoon salt (optional)

Preheat to 475 degrees.

Cut each potato into 8 wedges. Add to a large bowl along with the carrots and onions. Add remaining ingredients and toss to coat.

Arrange vegetables, so that they are not crowded, in a 9-inch by 13-inch baking pan that has been sprayed with non-stick cooking spray.

Roast 15 minutes.

Stir and turn vegetables. Return to oven for an additional 15 minutes or until vegetables are tender.

Note: One serving is a good source of fiber.

Cooking tip: Oven temperature can be lowered so these can bake along side another dish. Lowering the temperature will increase the cooking time.

Cheese Stuffed Potatoes

This is a potato dish that kids like. The addition of cheese adds a good flavor.

**4 medium baked potatoes, about 5 ounces each
(still warm)**
**1 cup low-fat cottage cheese or low-fat
Ricotta cheese**
1 tablespoon nonfat milk
2 tablespoons chopped green onion
1/4 teaspoon paprika

Slice each potato in half, lengthwise. Scoop out pulp, leaving about 1/4 inch thick shells.

Blend cheese, milk and potato pulp. Mash until smooth. Add onion.

Fill potato shell halves with mixture.

Arrange potatoes on a baking dish and sprinkle with paprika. Use a microwave-safe dish if cooking in microwave.

Follow directions below for microwave or conventional oven.

Microwave Oven: Cover with wax paper. Heat on high for 5 minutes, turning 1/4 turn halfway through cooking.

Conventional Oven: Prcheat oven to 350 degrees. Bake for 10-15 minutes or until thoroughly heated.

Makes 8 servings

Each Serving
1 potato half

Carb Servings
1

Exchanges
1 starch

Nutrient Analysis
calories 71
total fat 0g
saturated fat 0mg
cholesterol 1mg
sodium 120mg
total carbohydrate 12g
dietary fiber 2g
sugars 2g
protein 5g

This is easy to assemble and quick cooking if you're using a microwave. However, if you're not in a hurry, you'll find it is just as easy to use the oven. See the variation below for making this a main dish.

Makes 6 servings

Each Serving

Carb Servings
1 1/2

Exchanges
1 1/2 starch

Nutrient Analysis
calories 107
total fat 0g
saturated fat 0mg
cholesterol 1mg
sodium 62mg
total carbohydrate 22g
dietary fiber 3g
sugars 5g
protein 4g

Scalloped Potatoes

6-8 new potatoes, not peeled (about 4 cups, sliced)
2 tablespoons unbleached all-purpose flour
1 tablespoon dried or 1/4 cup fresh minced onion
1 teaspoon fat-free butter flavored sprinkles
1/4 teaspoon ground black pepper
1 1/2 cups nonfat milk

Spray a 2 1/2-quart casserole dish with non-stick cooking spray. Use a microwave-safe dish if cooking in the microwave.

Cut potatoes into 1/4-inch slices. Layer potatoes in the casserole, sprinkling each layer with flour, onion, butter sprinkles and pepper.

Pour milk over top.

Follow directions below for microwave or conventional oven.

Microwave Oven: Cook, covered, 15-18 minutes, stirring every 4 minutes. Be sure to use a container twice the size of the contents to prevent a boil over.

Conventional Oven: Preheat oven to 350 degrees. Bake uncovered about 1 1/4 hours. Stir two to three times during cooking.

Note: One serving is a good source of fiber.

Variation: *Scalloped Potatoes with Meat* - To make this a main dish, add cubed ham or smoked turkey sausage before cooking. Top with 2 ounces grated, reduced-fat cheese.

Low-Fat French Fries

**4 medium potatoes, not peeled
  (about 5 ounces each)
1 tablespoon oil (canola or olive)
salt to taste (optional)
malt vinegar to taste (optional)**

Preheat oven to 475 degrees.

Cut potatoes into half inch slices or strips.

Place potato slices in a plastic bag with oil and shake well to coat potatoes evenly.

Spray a baking sheet with non-stick cooking spray. Arrange potatoes in a single layer and bake for 30 minutes, or until golden brown, turning potatoes every 10 minutes.

Sprinkle with salt, and serve with malt vinegar.

Note: One serving is a good source of fiber.

Variation: Temperature can be decreased to 450 degrees and baking time increased to 40 minutes.

This is a favorite for children and adults that is so easy to prepare! The best part is these fries are low in fat.

Makes 4 servings

Each Serving

Carb Servings
1 1/2

Exchanges
1 1/2 starch
1/2 fat

Nutrient Analysis
calories 129
total fat 4g
saturated fat 0mg
cholesterol 0mg
sodium 8mg
total carbohydrate 22g
dietary fiber 3g
sugars 2g
protein 2g

You can use either yams or sweet potatoes. The yams have a bright orange color and a stronger flavor. The sweet potatoes have a white color and a milder flavor. We prefer the taste of the sweet potatoes.

Makes 4 servings

Each Serving

Carb Servings
1

Exchanges
1 1/2 starch
1/2 fat

Nutrient Analysis
calories 116
total fat 4g
saturated fat 0mg
cholesterol 0mg
sodium 15mg
total carbohydrate 20g
dietary fiber 3g
sugars 4g
protein 2g

Sweet Potato Fries

**4 medium sweet potatoes or yams, peeled
  (about 4 ounces each)
1 tablespoon oil (canola or olive)
salt to taste (optional)**

Preheat oven to 450 degrees.

Cut potatoes into half inch slices or strips.

Place potato slices in a plastic bag with oil and shake well to coat potatoes evenly.

Spray a baking sheet with non-stick cooking spray. Arrange potatoes in a single layer and bake for 12-15 minutes, or until golden brown, turning potatoes halfway through cooking.

Sprinkle with salt (optional).

Note: One serving is a good source of fiber.

Herb Rice Blend

1 1/2 cups fat-free beef or chicken broth*
1 teaspoon dried or 1 tablespoon fresh minced onion
1/4 teaspoon dried marjoram
1/4 teaspoon dried thyme
1/8 teaspoon dried rosemary
1 1/2 cups quick-cooking brown rice

Mix the first five ingredients in a saucepan. Bring to a boil. Add rice and reduce heat to low. Cover and simmer for 5 minutes. Remove from heat and let stand 5 minutes before serving.

*Sodium is figured for reduced-salt.

Variation: *Italian Herb Rice Blend* - Substitute 3/4 teaspoon Italian seasoning for the rosemary, marjoram and thyme.

Herb and Vegetable Rice Blend

1 recipe Herb Rice Blend (above)
1 cup cooked, sliced vegetables (such as mushrooms, celery, etc.)

Prepare one full recipe of Herb Rice Blend.

Add hot vegetables and mix well.

Makes 2 cups
4 servings

Each Serving
1/2 cup

Carb Servings
1 1/2

Exchanges
1 1/2 starch

Nutrient Analysis
calories 132
total fat 1g
saturated fat 0mg
cholesterol 0mg
sodium 150mg
total carbohydrate 25g
dietary fiber 2g
sugars 0g
protein 4g

Makes 3 cups
4 servings

Each Serving
3/4 cup

Carb Servings
2

Exchanges
1 1/2 starch
1 vegetable

Nutrient Analysis
calories 136
total fat 1g
saturated fat 0mg
cholesterol 0mg
sodium 151mg
total carbohydrate 26g
dietary fiber 2g
sugars 0g
protein 4g

Try this "dressed up"
version of baked beans.
It can be served as a
side dish or as a main
dish.

Ranch Beans

1 can (16 ounces) fat-free baked beans
1 can (15 ounces) red kidney beans,
**   drained**
1/2 cup chopped green pepper
2 tablespoons catsup
2 tablespoons molasses
1 tablespoon Dijon mustard
1/2 teaspoon dried or 2 teaspoons fresh
**   minced onion**

Stovetop: Place all ingredients in saucepan and heat thoroughly (about 10 minutes).

Microwave Oven: Place all ingredients in a microwave-safe bowl. Cover and cook on high for 5 minutes, stirring halfway through cooking time.

Note: One serving is an excellent source of fiber.

Makes 3 cups
6 servings

Each Serving
1/2 cup

Carb Servings*
1 1/2

Exchanges*
1 1/2 starch

Nutrient Analysis
calories 160
total fat 0g
saturated fat 0mg
cholesterol 0mg
sodium 472mg
total carbohydrate 31g
dietary fiber 9g
sugars 8g
protein 8g

*reflects carbohydrate
 minus fiber

Sandwiches and Pizza

Try these recipes for lunch or a quick supper.
Use whole grain breads to increase the fiber
in your diet.

Makes 4 sandwiches

Each Serving
1 sandwich

Carb Servings
2

Exchanges
2 starch
2 lean meat

Nutrient Analysis
calories 271
total fat 8g
saturated fat 3mg
cholesterol 41mg
sodium 497mg
total carbohydrate 31g
dietary fiber 4g
sugars 5g
protein 21g

Turkey French Dips

4 ounces cooked turkey slices
4 long whole grain rolls, 2 ounces each
4 ounces reduced-fat mozzarella cheese slices
1 package au jus gravy mix

Preheat oven to 400 degrees.

Cut rolls lengthwise. Place one ounce turkey and one ounce mozzarella cheese on each roll.

Wrap each roll in aluminum foil and heat in the oven for 10 minutes.

Prepare au jus according to package directions or add more water to reduce the sodium content.

Slice each sandwich in half, diagonally. Serve each with 1/3 cup au jus.

Note: One serving is a good source of fiber.

Tomato and Ricotta Sandwich

1 slice whole grain toast
1/4 cup low-fat Ricotta cheese
2 tomato slices
1/2 teaspoon Dijon mustard

Preheat broiler.

Spread cheese on toast. Top with tomato. Spread mustard on tomato. Broil until tomato is hot.

Note: One serving is a good source of fiber.

Meatball Sandwich

16 meatballs (page 219)
1 cup spaghetti sauce (less than 4 g fat
  per 4 ounces)
4 long whole grain rolls, 2 ounces each

Heat meatballs in spaghetti sauce.

Slice rolls lengthwise, being careful not to cut through the last half inch of the roll.

Fill each roll with 4 meatballs and 1/4 of the sauce.

Note: One serving is an excellent source of fiber.

This is especially quick to put together if you remember to thaw the bread dough overnight. Change the filling ingredients to suit your taste.

Crusty Calzone

Crust:
1 pound frozen whole wheat bread dough,
   thawed and at room temperature*
1/4 cup pizza sauce
1/2 teaspoon garlic powder
1/4 teaspoon Italian seasoning

Turkey Sausage Filling:
1/2 pound low-fat turkey smoked sausage,
   sliced very thin
1 green pepper, sliced
1/2 onion, sliced thin
1 cup (4 ounces) grated, reduced-fat cheese

Preheat oven to 425 degrees.

Roll dough into 10-inch by 14-inch rectangle. Place on a baking sheet that has been sprayed with non-stick cooking spray.

Spread pizza sauce on half of the dough. Sprinkle with garlic powder and Italian seasoning. Top with filling ingredients.

Fold dough over and press edges together to seal in filling.

Bake for 20 minutes.

Note: One serving is a good source of fiber.

*Thaw frozen bread dough in refrigerator overnight, then set out for about 1/2 hour at room temperature for easier rolling.

Individual Pizza

2 long whole grain rolls, 2 ounces each
1/2 cup pizza sauce
4 ounces cooked turkey slices
1/4 cup (1 ounce) grated, reduced-fat
  mozzarella cheese
1/4 cup (1 ounce) grated, reduced-fat
  cheddar cheese
1/4 cup thinly sliced green pepper
1/4 cup thinly sliced onion

Preheat oven to 475 degrees.

Cut rolls in half and spread pizza sauce over each half.

Top with turkey, cheeses and vegetables.

Bake for 15 minutes or until cheese is melted.

Note: One serving is a good source of fiber.

This is a quick pizza recipe. Try this one for lunch or as a quick after school snack.

Makes 4 pizzas

Each Serving
1 pizza

Carb Servings
1

Exchanges
1 starch
1/2 vegetable
1 1/2 lean meat

Nutrient Analysis
calories 167
total fat 4g
saturated fat 2mg
cholesterol 32mg
sodium 357mg
total carbohydrate 18g
dietary fiber 3g
sugars 4g
protein 15g

Makes 12 slices
6 servings

Each Serving
2 slices

Carb Servings*
2

Exchanges*
1 1/2 starch
2 vegetable
1 medium-fat meat

Nutrient Analysis
calories 252
total fat 7g
saturated fat 3mg
cholesterol 13mg
sodium 506mg
total carbohydrate 34g
dietary fiber 5g
sugars 6g
protein 14g

*reflects carbohydrate minus fiber

Piled High Vegetable Pizza

1 small eggplant, not peeled (about 12-14 ounces), cut into one-inch cubes (about 4 cups)
1 onion, chopped
1 cup chopped bell pepper, green or yellow
1 tablespoon chopped garlic
1 teaspoon Italian seasoning
1/2 teaspoon salt (optional)
1/4 teaspoon ground black pepper
2 medium tomatoes, chopped (about 2 cups)
1 (10 ounce) thin pizza crust (such as Boboli)
1/2 cup pizza sauce
1 cup (4 ounces) grated reduced-fat mozzarella cheese
1/4 cup Parmesan cheese (optional)

Preheat oven to 450 degrees.

In a large bowl, mix vegetables, except tomatoes, with garlic and seasonings. Spread in a 9-inch by 13-inch baking pan that has been sprayed with non-stick cooking spray.

Roast for 12-15 minutes. Add tomatoes and return to oven for 5 minutes or until all vegetables are tender. Drain any liquid.

While vegetables are roasting, place pizza crust on a baking pan. Spread pizza sauce over crust and top with cheese.

Bake for 8-10 minutes along side the vegetables. Top with roasted vegetables and Parmesan cheese.

Note: One serving is an excellent source of fiber.

Boboli Pizza Sausage Style

1 (10 ounce) thin pizza crust (such as Boboli)
1/2 cup pizza sauce
1 teaspoon Italian seasoning
1 cup (4 ounces) grated, reduced-fat cheese
    (mozzarella or cheddar)
6 ounces low-fat turkey smoked sausage

Preheat oven to 450 degrees.

Place pizza crust on pizza pan. Spoon on pizza sauce. Sprinkle with Italian seasoning and cheese.

Slice sausage extra thin and arrange over cheese.

Bake for 8-10 minutes or until cheese is melted.

Makes 12 slices
6 servings

Each Serving
2 slices

Carb Servings
2

Exchanges
1 1/2 starch
1/2 vegetable
1 1/2 medium-fat meat

Nutrient Analysis
calories 244
total fat 8g
saturated fat 3mg
cholesterol 28mg
sodium 720mg
total carbohydrate 26g
dietary fiber 1g
sugars 3g
protein 15g

Boboli Pizza Shrimp Style

1 (10 ounce) thin pizza crust (such as Boboli)
1/2 cup seafood cocktail sauce
1 cup (4 ounces) grated, reduced-fat cheese
    (mozzarella or cheddar)
2 cups cooked and cleaned shrimp

Preheat oven to 450 degrees.

Place pizza crust on pizza pan. Spread cocktail sauce on the pizza crust. Top with cheese. Bake for 5 minutes.

Top with shrimp and continue to cook for 3-5 minutes or until shrimp is heated and cheese is melted.

Makes 12 slices
6 servings

Each Serving
2 slices

Carb Servings
2

Exchanges
1 1/2 starch
1 vegetable
2 lean meat

Nutrient Analysis
calories 259
total fat 6g
saturated fat 2mg
cholesterol 110mg
sodium 708mg
total carbohydrate 28g
dietary fiber 1g
sugars 5g
protein 21g

Complete this meal by adding fresh fruit or a tossed salad. See the variation below for reducing calories and carbohydrate.

Makes 4 sandwiches

Each Serving
1 sandwich

Carb Servings
2

Exchanges
2 starch
3 lean meat

Nutrient Analysis
calories 321
total fat 10g
saturated fat 3mg
cholesterol 70mg
sodium 918mg
total carbohydrate 31g
dietary fiber 4g
sugars 7g
protein 27g

Sloppy Joes

1 pound extra lean ground beef or ground turkey (7% fat)
1/2 cup chopped onion
1 can (10 ounces) chicken gumbo soup, fat removed
1 tablespoon prepared mustard
1 tablespoon catsup
4 whole grain hamburger buns

Microwave Oven: In a microwave-safe bowl, crumble meat and add onion. Cook on high for 4 minutes, turning halfway through cooking time. Add soup, mustard and catsup. Continue cooking for about 2 minutes or until heated thoroughly.

Stovetop: Brown meat and onion in a skillet that has been sprayed with non-stick cooking spray. Add soup, mustard and catsup. Simmer for about 10 minutes.

Spoon meat mixture on 4 bun halves. Top with remaining buns.

For a crisp texture, place filled buns on a baking sheet and bake at 475 degrees for 5-10 minutes before serving.

Note: One serving is a good source of fiber.
This recipe is higher in sodium and should be limited by those on a low-sodium diet.

Variation: *Open-Faced Sloppy Joes* - Use only 2 hamburger buns. Spoon meat mixture on 4 bun halves and serve open-face. Serving size would be 1/2 bun with meat mixture. One serving: calories - 264, carbohydrate - 20g, carb servings - 1

Meatless Entrees

Use low-fat cheeses to cut back on fat and reduce calories. Egg substitute is a good choice for people advised to limit whole eggs. The addition of vegetables adds fiber to your diet.

You don't precook the noodles in this recipe so it is really fast to assemble. This can be put together the night before and refrigerated without baking. Increase baking time by 15 minutes if it has been refrigerated.

Makes 12 servings

Each Serving

Carb Servings
2

Exchanges
1 1/2 starch
1 vegetable
1 lean meat

Nutrient Analysis
calories 218
total fat 5g
saturated fat 2mg
cholesterol 9mg
sodium 596mg
total carbohydrate 28g
dietary fiber 2g
sugars 6g
protein 15g

Quick Lasagne

3 cups reduced-fat cottage cheese or reduced-fat Ricotta cheese
2 tablespoons dried parsley
1 teaspoon chopped garlic
4 cups spaghetti sauce (less than 4 g fat per 4 ounces)*
3/4 pound uncooked lasagne noodles (12 noodles)
1 cup (4 ounces) grated, reduced-fat mozzarella cheese
1/4 cup grated Parmesan cheese

Preheat oven to 350 degrees.

Spray a 9-inch by 13-inch baking pan with non-stick cooking spray.

Mix cottage cheese, parsley and garlic.

Pour 1 cup of sauce in bottom of pan.

Layer in this order: 4 noodles, 1/2 cheese mixture, 1/2 mozzarella, 1 cup sauce, 4 noodles, 1/2 cheese mixture, 1/2 mozzarella, 1 cup sauce, 4 noodles and the rest of the sauce. Sprinkle with Parmesan cheese.

Covered tightly with aluminum foil and bake for one hour.

*or one jar (1 pound, 10 ounces) and water to equal 4 cups

Puffy Chile Relleno Casserole

3 cans (7 ounces each) whole green chiles
5 whole wheat tortillas (8-inch), cut into
   1-inch strips
1 pound grated, reduced-fat cheese (cheddar
   or Mexican blend)
1/2 teaspoon each: ground black pepper, ground
   cumin, garlic powder
1/4 teaspoon salt (optional)
3 cups egg substitute (equal to 12 eggs)
3/4 cup nonfat milk
1 teaspoon paprika
salsa (optional)

Preheat oven to 350 degrees.

Spray a 9-inch by 13-inch baking pan with non-stick cooking spray.

Remove seeds from chiles. Lay half the chiles in the pan. Top with half the tortilla strips and then half of the cheese. Sprinkle with 1/2 of the seasonings (except the paprika).

Repeat another layer using remaining chiles, tortillas and cheese. Sprinkle with the remaining 1/2 of the seasonings (except the paprika).

Beat eggs with milk and pour over casserole. Sprinkle with paprika.

Bake uncovered for 40 minutes or until puffy and set in the center. Let sit 10 minutes before serving. Serve with salsa.

Note: One serving is a good source of fiber.

I like this recipe for brunch but it is also good for dinner. Serve it with sliced oranges and grapefruit sections. This recipe is higher in sodium and should be limited by those on a low-sodium diet.

Makes 8 servings

Each Serving

Carb Servings
1 1/2

Exchanges
1 starch
1 vegetable
3 lean meat

Nutrient Analysis
calories 290
total fat 10g
saturated fat 6mg
cholesterol 37mg
sodium 877mg
total carbohydrate 21g
dietary fiber 3g
sugars 4g
protein 27g

Fresh tomatoes and basil add a wonderful flavor to this light dish.

Tomato and Basil Pasta

4 medium tomatoes, diced (4 cups)
2 teaspoons dried basil
2 teaspoons chopped garlic
1 teaspoon salt (optional)
1/4 teaspoon ground black pepper
6 ounces angel hair pasta
grated Parmesan cheese (optional)

Mix the first five ingredients and let sit at room temperature at least one hour.

Cook angel hair pasta according to package directions and drain.

Top pasta with tomato mixture.

Serve immediately and top with Parmesan cheese (optional).

Note: One serving is a good source of fiber.

Makes 6 cups
4 servings

Each Serving
1 1/2 cups

Carb Servings
2 1/2

Exchanges
2 starch
2 vegetable

Nutrient Analysis
calories 193
total fat 1g
saturated fat 0mg
cholesterol 0mg
sodium 9mg
total carbohydrate 39g
dietary fiber 4g
sugars 6g
protein 8g

Italian Broccoli and Pasta

2 cups uncooked fettucini noodles (eggless)
2 cups broccoli florets
3 tablespoons chopped green onion
1 can (14 ounces) diced tomatoes,* not drained
1/2 teaspoon dried thyme
1/2 teaspoon dried oregano
1/2 teaspoon ground black pepper
2 teaspoons grated Parmesan cheese

Cook fettucini according to package directions and drain.

Spray a skillet with non-stick cooking spray. Add broccoli and onion and stir-fry for 3 minutes.

Add tomatoes and seasonings and simmer until heated throughout.

Spoon vegetable mixture over fettucini and top with Parmesan cheese.

*Sodium is figured for reduced-salt.

Note: One serving is a good source of fiber.

This has a great flavor. Try adding shrimp for variety.

Makes 4 servings

Each Serving

Carb Servings
1 1/2

Exchanges
1 starch
1 1/2 vegetable

Nutrient Analysis
calories 109
total fat 1g
saturated fat 0mg
cholesterol 1mg
sodium 41mg
total carbohydrate 22g
dietary fiber 3g
sugars 6g
protein 5g

Makes 5 servings

Each Serving

Carb Servings*
1 1/2

Exchanges*
1 starch
2 vegetable

Nutrient Analysis
calories 169
total fat 3g
saturated fat 1mg
cholesterol 0mg
sodium 616mg
total carbohydrate 29g
dietary fiber 5g
sugars 11g
protein 6g

***reflects carbohydrate minus fiber**

Vegetables Primavera

4 cups vegetables, any combination of the following:
  chopped: broccoli, cauliflower, celery, cabbage, eggplant, onions
  sliced: mushrooms, green peppers, carrots
  whole: pea pods, green beans
1 jar (26 ounces) spaghetti sauce (less than 4 g fat per 4 ounces)
2 1/2 cups cooked spaghetti noodles

Microwave Oven: Mix vegetables and spaghetti sauce in a microwave-safe dish. Cover and cook on high for 15 minutes, stirring at 5-minute intervals. Cook longer if you prefer vegetables to be less crisp.

Stovetop: Mix vegetables and spaghetti sauce in a saucepan. Cover and simmer until vegetables are cooked to preferred tenderness.

Serve cooked vegetables and sauce over noodles.

Note: One serving is an excellent source of fiber.

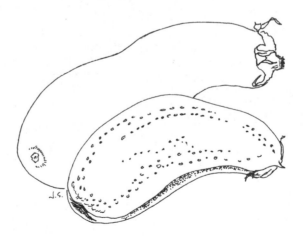

Italian Zucchini Frittata

This is a good way to use zucchini and it is a delicious supper or breakfast dish.

4 cups unpeeled, grated zucchini (about 1 1/2 pounds)
2 tablespoons chopped onion
1/2 teaspoon chopped garlic
1 cup egg substitute (equal to 4 eggs)
2 tablespoons nonfat milk
1/2 teaspoon dried oregano
1/2 teaspoon dried basil
1/2 teaspoon salt (optional)
1/4 teaspoon ground black pepper
2 tablespoons grated Parmesan cheese

Preheat broiler.

Spray a 10-inch skillet with non-stick cooking spray.

Sauté the first three ingredients until zucchini is tender, pouring off any liquid.

Meanwhile, mix eggs, milk and seasonings. Add to the zucchini mixture and cook until the eggs begin to set.

Top with Parmesan cheese. Broil just until top is golden.

Makes 4 servings

Each Serving

Carb Servings
1/2

Exchanges
1 vegetable
1 very lean meat

Nutrient Analysis
calories 65
total fat 1g
saturated fat 0mg
cholesterol 2mg
sodium 168mg
total carbohydrate 6g
dietary fiber 1g
sugars 3g
protein 9g

This is one of my favorite omelets. I like the combination of chiles, salsa and eggs.

Makes 4 servings

Each Serving

Carb Servings
1/2

Exchanges
1 vegetable
1 very lean meat

Nutrient Analysis
calories 59
total fat 0g
saturated fat 0mg
cholesterol 0mg
sodium 221mg
total carbohydrate 7g
dietary fiber 2g
sugars 3g
protein 8g

Spanish Zucchini Frittata

4 cups unpeeled, grated zucchini (about 1 1/2 pounds)
2 tablespoons chopped onion
1/2 teaspoon chopped garlic
1 can (4 ounces) diced green chiles
1 cup egg substitute (equal to 4 eggs)
2 tablespoons nonfat milk
1/2 teaspoon ground cumin
1/2 teaspoon chili powder
1/2 teaspoon salt (optional)
1/4 teaspoon ground black pepper
salsa (optional)

Preheat broiler.

Spray a 10-inch skillet with non-stick cooking spray.

Sauté the first three ingredients until zucchini is tender, pouring off any liquid. Add chiles.

Meanwhile, mix eggs, milk and seasonings. Add to the zucchini mixture and cook until the eggs begin to set.

Broil just until top is golden. Serve with salsa.

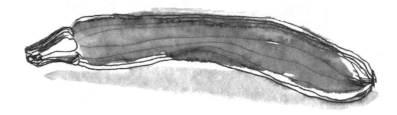

Poultry

Poultry is a lean choice if the skin and fat are removed. Keep some boneless, skinless pieces in the freezer for last minute meals.

This Asian dish has a unique flavor. Serve as an hors d'oeuvre, sandwich or as a main dish. The optional toppings of mint, green onion and peanuts allow you to individualize your wrap.

Makes 12 wraps
4 servings

Each Serving
3 wraps

Carb Servings
0

Exchanges
3 1/2 very lean meat

Nutrient Analysis
calories 131
total fat 2g
saturated fat 0mg
cholesterol 65mg
sodium 76mg
total carbohydrate 2g
dietary fiber 1g
sugars 0g
protein 26g

Chicken Lettuce Wraps

**1 pound skinless, boneless chicken breasts,
   cut into bite-size pieces
2 tablespoons minced fresh ginger
1/2 teaspoon salt (optional)
1/4 teaspoon ground black pepper
1/2 cup chopped fresh cilantro
12 large lettuce leaves (bib or butter)**

**Optional Toppings:
green onion, sliced
mint leaves, chopped
dry roasted peanuts, coarsely chopped**

In a medium saucepan, that has been sprayed with non-stick cooking spray, sauté chicken with ginger for a few minutes, until chicken is no longer pink. Season with salt and pepper. Add cilantro.

To serve, arrange a bowl of chicken mixture, lettuce leaves and optional toppings on serving area.

To make each lettuce wrap, place about 1/4 cup of chicken mixture in a lettuce leaf. Add optional toppings. Roll up and enjoy!

Variation:
Chicken Pitas: Cut 3 pocket breads in half. Line each with lettuce. Add 1/2 cup of chicken mixture to each pocket.

Cooked and Cubed Chicken

1 3/4 pounds boneless, skinless chicken breasts

Follow directions below for microwave or conventional oven.

Microwave Oven: Cut breasts into 1-inch strips. Arrange on a microwave-safe baking dish in a circle on the outer portion of the dish. Cover with wax paper and microwave on high for 5 minutes, rearranging halfway through cooking time. Let sit a few minutes before cutting into bite-size pieces.

Stovetop Method: Place chicken in a saucepan and cover with water. Cover and simmer on low until tender (about 15-20 minutes). Drain liquid and save for making soup. Cut into bite-size pieces.

Cooked and cubed chicken is used in the following recipes:
- Baked Chimichangas
- Cabbage and Chicken Salad
- Chicken and Biscuits
- Chicken and Fruit Salad
- Chicken and Spinach Salad
- Chicken Enchiladas
- Chicken in a Pocket
- Chicken Tortilla Casserole
- Chinese Chicken Salad
- Cinnamon Chicken Salad
- Green Chile Chicken Enchilada Casserole
- Oriental Rice and Chicken Salad

Many recipes call for cooked chicken. You can use leftover turkey or leftover chicken, but when leftovers are not available, it's easy to microwave or simmer chicken. Cook extra and freeze for future use.

Makes 4 cups
8 servings

Each Serving
1/2 cup

Carb Servings
0

Exchanges
3 very lean meat

Nutrient Analysis
calories 108
total fat 1g
saturated fat 0mg
cholesterol 57mg
sodium 64mg
total carbohydrate 0g
dietary fiber 0g
sugars 0g
protein 23g

Makes 10 pockets
5 servings

Each Serving
2 pockets

Carb Servings
3

Exchanges
3 starch
3 very lean meat

Nutrient Analysis
calories 367
total fat 6g
saturated fat 1mg
cholesterol 48mg
sodium 1257mg
total carbohydrate 49g
dietary fiber 3g
sugars 9g
protein 30g

Chicken in a Pocket

2 cups cooked chicken, chopped or shredded
1 package (8 ounces) nonfat cream cheese (room temperature)
4 green onions, chopped
2 cans (7 ounces each) buttermilk biscuits (10 biscuits per can)

Sauce:
1 can (10 ounces) reduced-fat cream of chicken soup*
1/2 can water

Preheat oven to 375 degrees.

Mix the first three ingredients in a medium bowl.

Lay out half the biscuits on a baking sheet that has been sprayed with non-stick cooking spray. Lightly flatten the biscuits with the palm of your hand.

Equally divide the chicken mixture on the ten biscuits. Flatten remaining biscuits and place over biscuits topped with filling. Seal edges by pinching.

Bake for 20 minutes or until biscuits are golden brown.

Meanwhile, prepare sauce by mixing the soup and water. Heat in a saucepan on the stove until thoroughly heated or cook in the microwave for two and a half minutes on high, stirring halfway through cooking time. Serve over each pocket.

*To reduce sodium, choose soups that are also 30% less sodium.

Note: One serving is a good source of fiber.
This recipe is higher in sodium and should be limited by those on a low-sodium diet.

Polynesian Chicken

**1 pound skinless, boneless chicken breasts or
    2 pounds chicken parts, with bone**
1/4 cup fat-free chicken broth,* or white wine
2 tablespoons lite soy sauce
2 tablespoons water
1 teaspoon liquid smoke
1/2 teaspoon ground ginger
**1/4 cup brown sugar or the equivalent in
    artificial sweetener**
1 teaspoon ground mustard

Skin chicken if parts are used.

Mix the next five ingredients. Add chicken and marinate
in the refrigerator for 1-3 hours.

Preheat oven to 350 degrees.

Add chicken and the marinade to a baking pan that has
been sprayed with non-stick cooking spray. Be sure the
pan is large enough so chicken pieces are not touching.
Top chicken pieces with brown sugar and mustard.

Bake for 30-40 minutes, or until chicken is no longer
pink, basting during the last 15 minutes of cooking
time. Serve with the sauce.

*Sodium is figured for reduced-salt.

The liquid smoke gives this dish an excellent flavor. The marinade becomes a delicious sauce that is especially good served over rice or noodles.

Makes 4 servings

Each Serving

Carb Servings
1 - with
    artificial sweetener 0

Exchanges
1 starch - 0 with
    artificial sweetener
3 1/2 very lean meat

Nutrient Analysis
calories 186 - with
    artificial sweetener 134
total fat 2g
saturated fat 0mg
cholesterol 65mg
sodium 389mg
total carbohydrate 14g - with
    artificial sweetener 1g
dietary fiber 0g
sugars 13g - with
    artificial sweetener 0g
protein 27g

This recipe is a complete meal. It is very colorful and a good choice to serve when entertaining. Try tube shaped or spiral pasta for variety.

Makes 9 cups
6 servings

Each Serving
1 1/2 cups

Carb Servings
1 1/2

Exchanges
1 1/3 starch
1 vegetable
2 1/2 very lean meat

Nutrient Analysis
calories 213
total fat 2g
saturated fat 0mg
cholesterol 43mg
sodium 89mg
total carbohydrate 25g
dietary fiber 3g
sugars 3g
protein 24g

Mediterranean Chicken

6 ounces pasta of your choice
1 pound skinless, boneless chicken breasts, cut
into bite-size pieces
1 tablespoon chopped garlic
8 ounces fresh sliced mushrooms (about 3 cups)
2 red bell peppers, chopped (about 2 cups)
2 cups broccoli florets, cut into bite-size pieces
1/2 teaspoon crushed red pepper
1/2 teaspoon Italian seasoning
1/4 teaspoon salt (optional)
1/8 teaspoon ground black pepper
1/2 cup fat-free chicken broth*
1 can (4 ounces) sliced black olives,
drained (optional)
1/2 cup nonfat feta cheese (optional)

Cook pasta according to package directions. Drain.

Meanwhile, spray a large skillet with non-stick cooking spray. Add chicken to skillet and cook until chicken is no longer pink. Remove from skillet and keep warm.

Add vegetables and seasonings to skillet. Stir-fry for about 4-5 minutes until crisp-tender. Add water or broth, as needed, to prevent sticking.

Add chicken, broth and hot noodles to vegetables. Toss well. Cover and let sit a couple of minutes before serving.

If desired, top with feta cheese.

*Sodium is figured for reduced-salt.

Note: One serving is a good source of fiber.

Chicken Breasts Florentine

2 tablespoons unbleached all-purpose flour
1/4 cup nonfat milk
3/4 cup fat-free chicken broth*
2 tablespoons grated Parmesan cheese
1/4 teaspoon salt (optional)
1/8 teaspoon ground black pepper
1/8 teaspoon ground nutmeg
2 packages (10 ounces each) frozen spinach,
**   thawed, drained and squeezed**
1 1/2 pounds skinless, boneless, chicken breasts,
**   cut into strips**

Preheat oven to 375 degrees.

Shake flour with milk in a covered container to prevent lumps. Mix flour mixture with chicken broth in a saucepan.

Bring to a boil, stirring constantly, until thickened. Take off heat and stir in Parmesan cheese, salt, pepper and nutmeg.

Mix spinach with 1/2 of the sauce and spread in a 9-inch by 13-inch baking pan that has been sprayed with non-stick cooking spray.

Arrange chicken over spinach. Pour remainder of sauce over chicken. Sprinkle with additional nutmeg.

Bake, uncovered, for 20-25 minutes or until chicken is no longer pink.

*Sodium is figured for reduced-salt.

This is a very simple and attractive dish. Fresh Parmesan cheese adds a good flavor to this recipe.

Makes 6 servings

Each Serving

Carb Servings
1/2

Exchanges
1 vegetable
4 very lean meat

Nutrient Analysis
calories 164
total fat 2g
saturated fat 1mg
cholesterol 67mg
sodium 205mg
total carbohydrate 6g
dietary fiber 2g
sugars 1g
protein 29g

Makes 5 servings

Each Serving

Carb Servings
1/2

Exchanges
2 vegetable
3 very lean meat

Nutrient Analysis
calories 168
total fat 3g
saturated fat 1mg
cholesterol 54mg
sodium 351mg
total carbohydrate 10g
dietary fiber 4g
sugars 3g
protein 25g

Chicken and Broccoli Casserole

1 pound skinless, boneless chicken breasts, cut into 8 strips
4 cups bite-size broccoli pieces
1 can (13 ounces) mushroom pieces and stems, drained
1 can (10 ounces) reduced-fat cream of mushroom soup*
1/4 can water
1/2 teaspoon dried rosemary
1/4 teaspoon paprika
1/8 teaspoon ground black pepper

Preheat oven to 350 degrees.

Arrange chicken in an 8-inch by 8-inch baking pan that has been sprayed with non-stick cooking spray. Top with vegetables.

Mix soup, water and rosemary. Spread over chicken and vegetables. Sprinkle with paprika and pepper.

Bake, uncovered, for 40-45 minutes or until chicken is no longer pink and broccoli is tender.

*To reduce sodium, choose soups that are also 30% less sodium.

Note: One serving is a good source of fiber.

Chicken and Vegetables in Gravy

1 1/2 pounds skinless, boneless chicken breasts or
   2 1/2 pounds-3 pounds chicken parts, skin
   removed
1 can (14 ounces) quartered artichoke hearts,
   drained or 2 cups of broccoli florets
1 can (13 ounces) mushroom pieces and stems,
   drained
1/2 teaspoon paprika
1/4 teaspoon ground black pepper
1 1/2 cups fat-free chicken broth,* divided
1/3 cup unbleached all-purpose flour
1/3 cup dry sherry or chicken broth*
1/2 teaspoon dried rosemary
1/2 teaspoon salt (optional)

Preheat oven to 350 degrees. If using chicken breasts, cut into strips.

Place chicken in a 9-inch by 13-inch baking pan that has been sprayed with non-stick cooking spray.

Arrange artichoke hearts and mushrooms between chicken pieces. Sprinkle paprika and pepper over chicken.

In a covered container, shake flour with 1/2 cup of cold broth to prevent lumps. In a saucepan, add flour/broth mixture, remaining broth, dry sherry, salt and rosemary.

Heat on medium and bring to a boil, stirring constantly until thickened. Pour over chicken and bake for 40-50 minutes.

*Sodium is figured for reduced-salt.

Note: One serving is a good source of fiber.

The artichokes give a tangy flavor or you can substitute broccoli. This makes a very good mushroom gravy.

Makes 6 servings
___

Each Serving

Carb Servings
1

Exchanges
1/2 starch
1 vegetable
3 1/2 very lean meat

Nutrient Analysis
calories 192
total fat 2g
saturated fat 0mg
cholesterol 65mg
sodium 337mg
total carbohydrate 11g
dietary fiber 4g
sugars 1g
protein 30g

This is a very easy one-dish meal. Look for biscuits that are only 100 calories, 1.5grams of fat and 1gram of fiber for 2 biscuits. This recipe is good for using leftover turkey or chicken.

Makes 5 servings

Each Serving

Carb Servings
2

Exchanges
1 1/2 starch
1 vegetable
3 very lean meat

Nutrient Analysis
calories 257
total fat 3g
saturated fat 1mg
cholesterol 44mg
sodium 581mg
total carbohydrate 32g
dietary fiber 4g
sugars 7g
protein 25g

Chicken and Biscuits

3 tablespoons unbleached all-purpose flour
1 1/4 cups fat-free chicken broth,* divided
1/2 cup nonfat milk
2 cups cooked chicken, cubed
1 cup frozen peas, thawed
**1 can (13 ounces) mushroom pieces and
   stems, drained**
1 jar (2 ounces) chopped pimiento, drained
dash ground black pepper
**1 can (7 ounces) buttermilk biscuits
   (10 biscuits per can)**
1 teaspoon dried parsley

Preheat oven to 375 degrees.

In a small covered container, shake flour with 1/2 cup of broth.

In a medium saucepan that has been sprayed with non-stick cooking spray, add remaining broth, milk and flour mixture.

Bring to a boil, stirring constantly until thickened. Reduce heat and add chicken, peas, mushrooms, pimiento and pepper. Simmer, stirring occasionally, until heated throughout.

In a 2-quart casserole that has been sprayed with non-stick cooking spray, add hot chicken mixture.
Place biscuits on top of the hot chicken mixture.
Sprinkle with parsley.

Bake 20 minutes or until biscuits are golden brown.

*Sodium is figured for reduced-salt.

Note: One serving is a good source of fiber.

Chicken and Artichokes Dijon

Dijon sauce:
1/4 cup light mayonnaise
3 tablespoons nonfat plain yogurt
1 tablespoon Dijon mustard
2 teaspoons sugar or the equivalent in
    artificial sweetener
1 teaspoon dried parsley
1/4 teaspoon ground black pepper

1 cup uncooked quick-cooking brown rice
1 cup fat-free chicken broth*
1 pound skinless, boneless chicken breasts, cut
    into strips
1 cup chopped red bell pepper
1 can (14 ounces) quartered artichoke hearts,
    drained

Preheat oven to 350 degrees.

Mix mayonnaise, yogurt, mustard, sugar and seasonings to make the sauce. Set aside.

Spread rice in the bottom of a 2-quart covered casserole that has been sprayed with non-stick cooking spray. Pour broth over rice.

Arrange chicken and vegetables over rice.

Cover and bake for 45 minutes. Top with sauce. Return to oven, uncovered, for 5 minutes.

*Sodium is figured for reduced-salt.

Note: One serving is an excellent source of fiber.

The rich tasting Dijon sauce combined with the artichoke hearts gives a delightful flavor to this recipe. It's a good choice for company.

Makes 4 servings

Each Serving

Carb Servings*
1 1/2

Exchanges*
1 starch
1 vegetable
3 1/2 very lean meat
1/2 fat

Nutrient Analysis
calories 316 - with
    artificial sweetener 308
total fat 7g
saturated fat 1mg
cholesterol 70mg
sodium 471mg
total carbohydrate 28g - with
    artificial sweetener 26g
dietary fiber 5g
sugars 5g - with
    artificial sweetener 3g
protein 31g

***reflects carbohydrate
 minus fiber**

Makes 4 servings

Each Serving

Carb Servings
1 1/2

Exchanges
1 starch
2 vegetable
3 very lean meat

Nutrient Analysis
calories 247
total fat 2g
saturated fat 0mg
cholesterol 65mg
sodium 231mg
total carbohydrate 25g
dietary fiber 4g
sugars 4g
protein 29g

Chicken and Rice Casserole

1 cup uncooked quick-cooking brown rice
1 pound skinless, boneless chicken breasts,
**   cut into bite-size pieces**
1 1/2 cups sliced baby carrots
1 cup sliced celery
1/2 cup chopped onion
1 cup fat-free chicken broth*
1 teaspoon chopped garlic
1 teaspoon Italian seasoning
1/4 teaspoon salt (optional)
1/8 teaspoon ground black pepper

Preheat oven to 350 degrees.

Spray a covered 2-quart casserole with non-stick cooking spray.

Spread rice in the casserole. Top rice with chicken and vegetables.

Mix seasonings with broth. Pour over chicken mixture. Cover and bake for 45 minutes.

Let sit ten minutes before serving.

*Sodium is figured for reduced-salt.

Note: One serving is a good source of fiber.

Chicken Breasts in Mushroom Sauce

2 cups sliced mushrooms
1/4 cup chopped green onion
2 tablespoons unbleached all-purpose flour
1/4 cup water
1/2 cup nonfat plain yogurt
2 tablespoons dry sherry or water
1 teaspoon instant chicken bouillon*
1/4 teaspoon salt (optional)
1/8 teaspoon ground black pepper
1 pound skinless, boneless chicken breasts
1/4 teaspoon paprika

Preheat oven to 350 degrees.

Sauté mushrooms and onion in a skillet that has been sprayed with a non-stick cooking spray.

Mix flour and water in a covered container and shake well to prevent lumps. Add to mushrooms along with next five ingredients. Cook, stirring constantly, until thickened.

Arrange chicken in a 9-inch by 9-inch baking dish that has been sprayed with non-stick cooking spray.

Pour mushroom sauce over chicken and sprinkle with paprika.

Bake for 30 minutes or until chicken is no longer pink.

*Sodium is figured for reduced-salt.

The sherry and yogurt add a good flavor to this recipe. The sauce is good over brown rice, potatoes or noodles.

Makes 4 servings

Each Serving

Carb Servings
1/2

Exchanges
1/2 starch
3 1/2 very lean meat

Nutrient Analysis
calories 170
total fat 2g
saturated fat 0mg
cholesterol 66mg
sodium 152mg
total carbohydrate 8g
dietary fiber 1g
sugars 3g
protein 29g

Makes 6 servings

Each Serving

Carb Servings
0

Exchanges
1/4 starch
3 1/2 very lean meat

Nutrient Analysis
calories 137
total fat 1g
saturated fat 0mg
cholesterol 65mg
sodium 100mg
total carbohydrate 3g
dietary fiber 0g
sugars 0g
protein 26g

Oven Fried Chicken

1/4 cup cornflake crumbs
1/4 teaspoon dried thyme
1/4 teaspoon dried sage
1/8 teaspoon salt (optional)
1/8 teaspoon ground black pepper
1 1/2 pounds skinless, boneless chicken breasts or
    2 1/2 pounds - 3 pounds chicken parts

Skin chicken if parts are used.

Preheat oven to 425 degrees.

Spray a 9-inch by 13-inch baking pan with non-stick cooking spray.

Mix the first five ingredients in a plastic bag. Place a few pieces of chicken at a time in the plastic bag and shake to coat evenly.

Arrange chicken pieces in the pan so that they are not touching.

Bake boneless chicken breasts for 15-20 minutes and chicken parts for 45-60 minutes.

Variation: *Italian Oven Fried Chicken* – Substitute 1/2 teaspoon of Italian seasoning for the dried sage and dried thyme.

Chicken Nuggets

1/2 cup cornflake crumbs
1/2 teaspoon dried thyme
1/2 teaspoon dried sage
1/4 teaspoon salt (optional)
1/8 teaspoon ground black pepper
1 pound skinless, boneless chicken breasts
assorted mustards (optional)

Mix the first five ingredients in a plastic bag and set aside.

Cut chicken into bite-size pieces. Place a few pieces of chicken at a time in the plastic bag and shake to coat evenly. Follow directions below for microwave or conventional oven.

Microwave Oven: Arrange chicken pieces, so they are not touching, in a 9-inch by 13-inch glass baking dish that has been sprayed with non-stick cooking spray. Cover with wax paper and cook on high for 6-8 minutes or until chicken is cooked, rearranging twice during cooking time.

Conventional Oven: Preheat oven to 425 degrees. Arrange chicken pieces, so they are not touching, in a baking pan that has been sprayed with non-stick cooking spray. Bake for 12-14 minutes.

Optional mustards for dipping:
sweet and sour - 25 calories per tablespoon
honey mustard - 35 calories per tablespoon
hot mustard (prepared) or dry mustard (follow package
   directions to mix with water) - 10 calories per tablespoon

Variation: *Italian Chicken Nuggets* – Substitute 1 teaspoon of Italian seasoning for the dried sage and dried thyme.

These are a favorite for children. Serve with the Low-Fat French Fries recipe in this book. You can find cornflake crumbs in the breadings section of the grocery store.

Makes 4 servings

Each Serving

Carb Servings
1/2

Exchanges
2/3 starch
3 1/2 very lean meat

Nutrient Analysis
calories 164
total fat 1g
saturated fat 0mg
cholesterol 65mg
sodium 153mg
total carbohydrate 9g
dietary fiber 0g
sugars 1g
protein 27g

This is a special way to serve chicken. It is so moist and flavorful. You can find cornflake crumbs in the breadings section of the grocery store.

Makes 8 servings

Each Serving

Carb Servings
1/2

Exchanges
1/2 starch
3 1/2 very lean meat

Nutrient Analysis
calories 162
total fat 1g
saturated fat 0mg
cholesterol 65mg
sodium 138mg
total carbohydrate 6g
dietary fiber 0g
sugars 1g
protein 27g

Chicken Breasts Supreme

1/2 cup cornflake crumbs
1/2 teaspoon dried thyme
1/2 teaspoon dried sage
1/4 teaspoon salt (optional)
1/8 teaspoon ground black pepper
2 pounds skinless, boneless chicken breasts
1/2 cup sliced onion
1/2 cup fat-free chicken broth*
1/2 cup dry white wine, vermouth or chicken broth
2 cups mushrooms, sliced

Preheat oven to 375 degrees.

Mix the first five ingredients in a plastic bag. Place a couple pieces of chicken at a time in the plastic bag and shake to coat evenly.

Arrange chicken in a 9-inch by 13-inch baking pan that has been sprayed with non-stick cooking spray.

Spray a skillet with non-stick cooking spray and sauté onions. Add broth and wine. Bring to a boil. Pour around chicken.

Bake, uncovered, for 30 minutes.

Meanwhile, in the same skillet, sauté mushrooms. Arrange mushrooms around chicken after the chicken has cooked for 30 minutes.

Bake an additional 10 minutes or until chicken is no longer pink.

*Sodium is figured for reduced-salt.

Crispy Potato Chicken

If you like hash browns, you'll like this dish.

1 pound skinless, boneless chicken breasts
2 tablespoons Dijon mustard
1/2 teaspoon chopped garlic
2 new potatoes, not peeled (about 5 ounces, total)
1 teaspoon oil (canola or olive)
1/4 teaspoon lemon juice*
1 teaspoon ground black pepper

Preheat oven to 425 degrees.

Arrange chicken in a 9-inch by 9-inch baking dish that has been sprayed with non-stick cooking spray.

Mix mustard and garlic. Spread over chicken.

Grate potatoes and mix with oil and lemon juice. Spread over chicken. Sprinkle with pepper.

Bake for 25-35 minutes until chicken is no longer pink and potatoes are golden brown.

*Lemon juice is used to prevent the potatoes from turning gray.

Makes 4 servings

Each Serving

Carb Servings
1/2

Exchanges
1/2 starch
3 1/2 very lean meat

Nutrient Analysis
calories 167
total fat 3g
saturated fat 0mg
cholesterol 65mg
sodium 255mg
total carbohydrate 6g
dietary fiber 1g
sugars 0g
protein 27g

Makes 4 servings

Each Serving

Carb Servings
0

Exchanges
1/3 fruit
3 1/2 very lean meat

Nutrient Analysis
calories 143
total fat 2g
saturated fat 0mg
cholesterol 65mg
sodium 89mg
total carbohydrate 5g
dietary fiber 0g
sugars 1g
protein 27g

Yogurt Cumin Chicken

1 pound skinless, boneless chicken breasts
1/3 cup nonfat plain yogurt
3 tablespoons sugar-free apricot preserves
1 teaspoon ground cumin
1/2 teaspoon salt (optional)

Choose from one of the three methods below for cooking.

Conventional Oven: Preheat oven to 350 degrees. Arrange chicken in a baking pan that has been sprayed with non-stick cooking spray. Bake, uncovered, for 20 minutes. Drain any liquid. Mix remaining ingredients and spoon over chicken. Bake for 10 minutes or until chicken is no longer pink and sauce is heated.

Microwave Oven: Arrange chicken in a microwave-safe dish. Cover with plastic wrap, venting one corner. Cook on high for 6-8 minutes, or until chicken is no longer pink, rotating 1/4 turn halfway through cooking time. Drain any liquid. Mix remaining ingredients and spoon over chicken. Cook for 1-2 minutes or until sauce is heated.

Broiler or Barbecue Method: Cut 3 shallow slits lengthwise in each chicken breast half. Place slit side down on broiler pan. Mix remaining ingredients. Spoon half on chicken. Broil 3-4 inches from heat for 4 minutes. Turn chicken over and spoon on remaining yogurt mixture. Broil 5 minutes longer or until chicken is no longer pink.

French Glazed Chicken

1/4 cup nonfat French dressing
2 tablespoons sugar-free apricot preserves
2 tablespoons water
1 tablespoon dried or 1/4 cup fresh minced onion
1 pound skinless, boneless chicken breasts

Mix the first four ingredients and set aside.

Arrange chicken in a 9-inch by 9-inch baking pan that has been sprayed with non-stick cooking spray. Use a microwave-safe dish if cooking in the microwave.

Follow directions below for microwave or conventional oven.

Conventional Oven: Preheat oven to 350 degrees. Bake, uncovered, for 20 minutes. Drain any liquid. Spoon apricot mixture over chicken. Return to oven for 10 minutes or until chicken is no longer pink and glaze is heated.

Microwave Oven: Cover with plastic wrap, venting one corner. Cook on high for 6-8 minutes, or until chicken is no longer pink. Rotate 1/4 turn halfway through cooking. Drain any liquid. Spoon apricot mixture over chicken. Cook for 1-2 minutes or until glaze is heated.

The orange glaze adds color as well as flavor to the chicken. This same glaze is used in French Glazed Fish.

Makes 4 servings

Each Serving

Carb Servings
1/2

Exchanges
1/2 fruit
3 1/2 very lean meat

Nutrient Analysis
calories 155
total fat 1g
saturated fat 0mg
cholesterol 65mg
sodium 223mg
total carbohydrate 9g
dietary fiber 0g
sugars 3g
protein 26g

Makes 4 servings

Each Serving

Carb Servings
1/2

Exchanges
1 vegetable
3 1/2 very lean meat

Nutrient Analysis
calories 151
total fat 2g
saturated fat 0mg
cholesterol 65mg
sodium 82mg
total carbohydrate 6g
dietary fiber 3g
sugars 2g
protein 28g

Rolled Chicken and Asparagus

1 pound skinless, boneless chicken breasts
24 to 30 asparagus spears (tough ends removed)
2 tablespoons lemon juice
6 green onions, chopped
1/2 teaspoon salt (optional)
1/2 teaspoon ground black pepper

Preheat oven to 350 degrees.

Cut chicken breasts into 8 or 10 strips, each about 1-inch by 5-inches long.

Wrap each strip in a corkscrew fashion around 2 or 3 uncooked asparagus spears. Fasten with toothpicks.

Place in a covered baking dish that has been sprayed with non-stick cooking spray. Sprinkle with lemon juice, green onions, salt and pepper.

Cover and bake 25-30 minutes or until chicken is no longer pink. Remove toothpicks.

Serve hot or refrigerate until chilled and serve cold.

Note: One serving is a good source of fiber.

Chicken Picadillo

1 pound skinless, boneless chicken breasts
1 teaspoon ground cumin
3/4 cup salsa, thick and chunky
1/2 teaspoon chopped garlic
1 medium onion, sliced
1 medium green pepper, sliced

Cut chicken into 1-inch strips. Sprinkle with cumin.

Spray skillet with non-stick cooking spray.

Stir-fry chicken until tender and no longer pink.

Add salsa, garlic, onion and green pepper.

Cover and simmer for 10 minutes or until vegetables are tender.

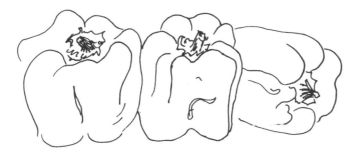

Serve this in a whole wheat tortilla or with a whole grain roll. It is also good served with brown rice. To reduce the sodium, use the salsa recipe in this book.

Makes 4 servings

Each Serving

Carb Servings
1/2

Exchanges
2 vegetable
3 1/2 very lean meat

Nutrient Analysis
calories 165
total fat 2g
saturated fat 0mg
cholesterol 65mg
sodium 297mg
total carbohydrate 9g
dietary fiber 1g
sugars 4g
protein 27g

Makes 4 servings

Each Serving

Carb Servings
0

Exchanges
1 vegetable
3 1/2 very lean meat

Nutrient Analysis
calories 138
total fat 1g
saturated fat 0mg
cholesterol 65mg
sodium 293mg
total carbohydrate 3g
dietary fiber 0g
sugars 2g
protein 26g

Chicken in Salsa

1 pound skinless, boneless chicken breasts
3/4 cup salsa

Arrange chicken in a 9-inch by 9-inch baking pan that has been sprayed with non-stick cooking spray.
Use a microwave-safe dish if cooking in the microwave.

Follow directions below for microwave or conventional oven.

Conventional Oven: Preheat oven to 350 degrees. Bake, uncovered, for 20 minutes. Spoon salsa over chicken. Return to oven for 10 minutes or until chicken is no longer pink and salsa is heated.

Microwave Oven: Cover with plastic wrap, venting one corner. Cook on high for 6-8 minutes, or until chicken is no longer pink. Rotate 1/4 turn halfway through cooking time. Drain any liquid. Spoon salsa over chicken. Cook for 1-2 minutes or until salsa is heated.

Chicken Fajitas

3 tablespoons lime juice
1/2 teaspoon coriander
1/2 teaspoon chili powder
1 pound skinless, boneless chicken breasts,
   cut into 1-inch strips
1 medium green pepper, sliced
1 medium onion, sliced
4 (8-inch) or 8 (6-inch) whole wheat tortillas
salsa (optional)

Mix lime juice with coriander and chili powder. Pour over chicken. Add sliced vegetables.

Spray skillet with non-stick cooking spray. Stir-fry chicken and vegetables until chicken is no longer pink and vegetables are crisp-tender.

Warm tortillas in microwave about 50 seconds on high or in a non-stick skillet.

Fill each tortilla with chicken mixture and serve with salsa and nonfat sour cream or nonfat yogurt.

Note: One serving is a good source of fiber.

This is a good family recipe. Serve with nonfat refried beans.

Makes 4 servings

Each Serving

Carb Servings
2

Exchanges
1 2/3 starch
1 vegetable
3 1/2 very lean meat

Nutrient Analysis
calories 278
total fat 3g
saturated fat 0mg
cholesterol 65mg
sodium 280mg
total carbohydrate 30g
dietary fiber 3g
sugars 6g
protein 32g

Makes 4 servings

Each Serving

Carb Servings
2

Exchanges
1 1/2 starch
1 vegetable
2 1/2 very lean meat

Nutrient Analysis
calories 260
total fat 5g
saturated fat 2mg
cholesterol 50mg
sodium 544mg
total carbohydrate 27g
dietary fiber 2g
sugars 5g
protein 24g

Baked Chimichangas

4 (8-inch) or 8 (6-inch) whole wheat tortillas

Filling:
1 1/2 cups cooked and cubed chicken
3/4 cup salsa, thick and chunky
1/2 cup (2 ounces) grated, reduced-fat cheddar
   or Mexican blend cheese
Optional: extra salsa
   Spanish Yogurt Sauce (page 68)

Preheat oven to 400 degrees.

Mix filling ingredients in a medium bowl.

Warm tortillas until pliable (about 5 seconds each in microwave or in a non-stick skillet).

Wet one side of tortilla and place wet side down. Spoon on filling ingredients. Fold to hold in filling.

Spray baking dish with non-stick cooking spray. Lay chimichangas, seam side down, on baking dish.

Bake for 15 minutes.

Variations: *Beef, Pork or Turkey Chimichangas* - Substitute ground or diced beef, pork, or turkey for chicken.

Chicken Tortilla Casserole

2 cans (10 ounces each) reduced-fat cream of chicken soup*
1 can of water
1 can (7 ounces) diced green chiles
1/4 cup dried or 1 cup fresh minced onion
1 teaspoon ground cumin
1/2 teaspoon chili powder
9 whole wheat tortillas (8-inch), cut into 1-inch strips
4 cups cooked and cubed chicken
1 cup (4 ounces) grated, reduced-fat cheddar cheese

Preheat oven to 350 degrees.

Combine soup with water. Add the next four ingredients and set aside.

Spray a 9-inch by 13-inch baking pan with non-stick cooking spray.

Place one third of the tortilla strips in the pan. Top with 1/2 the chicken, 1/3 of the soup mixture. Repeat layering with 1/3 of the tortilla strips, remaining chicken, 1/3 of the soup mixture, remaining tortillas and remaining soup mixture.

Bake uncovered for 35-40 minutes.

Top with cheese and bake for another 5 minutes.

*To reduce sodium, choose soups that are 30% less sodium.

Note: One serving is a good source of fiber.

This is a popular dish to take to potlucks. It is also a good way to use leftover chicken or turkey. Serve it with salsa or the Spanish Yogurt Sauce recipe in this book.

Makes 10 servings

Each Serving

Carb Servings
2

Exchanges
2 starch
3 very lean meat

Nutrient Analysis
calories 274
total fat 6g
saturated fat 2mg
cholesterol 55mg
sodium 570mg
total carbohydrate 30g
dietary fiber 3g
sugars 4g
protein 25g

Makes 8 servings

Each Serving

Carb Servings
2

Exchanges
1 starch
2 vegetable
3 lean meat

Nutrient Analysis
calories 281
total fat 8g
saturated fat 2mg
cholesterol 63mg
sodium 822mg
total carbohydrate 27g
dietary fiber 2g
sugars 4g
protein 27g

Green Chile Chicken Enchilada Casserole

1 can (28 ounces) green chile enchilada sauce, divided
4 cups cooked and cubed chicken
1/2 cup nonfat sour cream
1 can (7 ounces) diced green chiles
1/4 cup dried or 1 cup fresh minced onions
1 cup (4 ounces) grated, reduced-fat cheddar or Mexican cheese, divided
12 corn tortillas (6-inch)

Preheat oven to 350 degrees.

Combine 1 1/2 cups of enchilada sauce with chicken, sour cream, chiles, onions, and 1/2 cup of grated cheese. Set aside.

Spray a 9-inch by 13-inch baking pan with non-stick cooking spray.

Place one third of the tortillas in the pan, tearing tortillas to fill any empty areas. Top with 1/2 of the chicken mixture. Add another layer of the tortillas, top with remaining chicken mixture, and remaining tortillas. Pour remaining enchilada sauce over all.

Bake uncovered for 40 minutes.

Top with remaining grated cheese and return to oven for five minutes.

Note: This recipe is higher in sodium and should be limited by those on a low-sodium diet.

Chicken Enchiladas

2 cups cooked and cubed chicken
1 cup chopped onion
1 cup low-fat cottage cheese or Ricotta cheese
1 cup nonfat plain yogurt
1/2 cup (2 ounces) grated, reduced-fat cheddar or
   Mexican blend cheese
1/2 cup (2 ounces) grated, reduced-fat mozzarella
   cheese
2 cans (10 ounces each) enchilada sauce, divided
12 corn tortillas (6-inch)

Preheat oven to 375 degrees.

Mix the first six ingredients and set aside.

Spray a 9-inch by 13-inch baking dish with non-stick cooking spray. Pour 1/2 can of enchilada sauce in bottom of pan.

Follow either method below for layered or rolled.

Bake for 20-30 minutes or until heated thoroughly.

Rolled Method: Place about 1/3 to 1/2 cup of filling on each tortilla and roll to enclose (cracks in tortillas are not as noticeable after cooking). Place seam side down in baking dish. Top with remaining sauce.

Layered Method: Layer in this order: 1/3 of the tortillas, 1/2 of the filling, 1/3 tortillas, 1 can of sauce, remainder of filling, remainder of tortillas, remainder of sauce.

Note: One serving is a good source of fiber.

Variations: *Turkey, Pork or Beef Enchiladas* - Substitute 2 cups of ground or shredded meat for the chicken.

This recipe can be layered to save time or you can fill each tortilla and roll in the traditional way. Turkey, pork or beef can be substituted for the chicken.

Makes 8 servings

Each Serving

Carb Servings
2

Exchanges
1 1/2 starch
1 vegetable
2 lean meat

Nutrient Analysis
calories 237
total fat 6g
saturated fat 2mg
cholesterol 40mg
sodium 757mg
total carbohydrate 26g
dietary fiber 3g
sugars 4g
protein 19g

This is another complete meal in a pot. Serve with a dollop of nonfat yogurt or nonfat sour cream.

Makes 5 servings

Each Serving

Carb Servings
1 1/2

Exchanges
1 starch
2 vegetable
3 very lean meat

Nutrient Analysis
calories 241
total fat 4g
saturated fat 2mg
cholesterol 59mg
sodium 221mg
total carbohydrate 25g
dietary fiber 3g
sugars 6g
protein 27g

Mexican Style Chicken and Rice

1 cup uncooked quick-cooking brown rice
1 pound skinless, boneless chicken breasts, cut into bite-size pieces
1 medium onion, chopped (about 1 cup)
1 medium green pepper, chopped (about 1 cup)
1 can (14 ounces) diced tomatoes*
1 can (4 ounces) diced green chiles
1/2 cup water
1 teaspoon chopped garlic
1/2 teaspoon ground cumin
3 drops Tabasco sauce
1/4 teaspoon salt (optional)
1/8 teaspoon ground black pepper
1/2 cup (2 ounces) grated, reduced-fat cheddar cheese or reduced-fat Mexican cheese

Preheat oven to 350 degrees.

Spray a covered 2-quart casserole with non-stick cooking spray.

Spread rice in the casserole. Top with chicken, onion and green pepper.

Mix tomatoes, chiles, water and seasonings. Pour over chicken mixture.

Cover and bake for 45 minutes.

Top with cheese and return to oven for 5 minutes or until cheese is melted.

*Sodium is figured for reduced-salt.

Note: One serving is a good source of fiber.

Grilled Chicken with Coconut-Cilantro Sauce

1 can (13 ounces) light coconut milk
4 sliced green onions
3 tablespoons minced fresh ginger
2 tablespoons lite soy sauce
2 tablespoons brown sugar or the equivalent
   in artificial sweetener
2 tablespoons fresh lime juice
2 teaspoons chopped garlic
1 teaspoon ground fresh chili paste
1 cup chopped fresh cilantro
2 pounds skinless, boneless chicken breasts,
   cut into strips

In a small saucepan combine the first eight ingredients. Simmer for 5 minutes.

Barbecue: When barbecue is hot, place chicken on grill. Spoon a couple of tablespoons of coconut sauce over chicken. Cook about 4 minutes on each side or until chicken is no longer pink.

Conventional Oven: Preheat oven to 350 degrees. Place chicken in a 9-inch by 13-inch baking pan that has been sprayed with non-stick cooking spray. Spoon a couple of tablespoons of coconut sauce over chicken. Bake for 20-30 minutes or until chicken is no longer pink.

Add fresh cilantro to the sauce just before serving. Serve chicken with warm coconut-cilantro sauce.

The flavor of the coconut milk combined with fresh ginger and cilantro makes this Asian barbecue especially delicious. Light coconut milk has 60% less calories and fat than regular coconut milk.

Makes 8 servings

Each Serving

Carb Servings
1/2 - with
   artificial sweetener 0

Exchanges
1 vegetable
3 1/2 very lean meat

Nutrient Analysis
calories 178 - with
   artificial sweetener 165
total fat 4g
saturated fat 3mg
cholesterol 65mg
sodium 247mg
total carbohydrate 7g - with
   artificial sweetener 3g
dietary fiber 0g
sugars 4g - with
   artificial sweetener 1g
protein 27g

This is a great recipe for a summer barbecue but can also be prepared in the oven. This salsa is especially flavorful.

Makes 8 servings

Each Serving

Carb Servings
1/2

Exchanges
1 vegetable
3 1/2 very lean meat

Nutrient Analysis
calories 154
total fat 2g
saturated fat 0mg
cholesterol 65mg
sodium 85mg
total carbohydrate 7g
dietary fiber 1g
sugars 4g
protein 27g

Grilled Chicken with Corn Salsa

Corn Salsa
1 can (14 ounces) stewed tomatoes* or
   1 1/2 cups chopped fresh tomato
1 can (8 ounces) whole kernel corn,* drained
1 cup chopped cucumber, not peeled
1/2 cup chopped bell pepper, red or green
1/4 cup chopped fresh cilantro
2 tablespoons red wine vinegar
1/2 teaspoon each: garlic powder and ground cumin
1/4 teaspoon salt (optional)
1/8 teaspoon ground black pepper
1/8 teaspoon cayenne pepper

2 pounds skinless, boneless chicken breasts,
   cut into strips
1/4 teaspoon salt (optional)
1/8 teaspoon ground black pepper

Combine salsa ingredients and set aside.

Barbecue: When barbecue is hot, place chicken on grill. Season with salt and pepper. Cook about 4 minutes on each side or until chicken is no longer pink.

Conventional Oven: Preheat oven to 350 degrees. Place chicken in a 9-inch by 13-inch baking pan that has been sprayed with non-stick cooking spray. Season with salt and pepper. Bake for 20-30 minutes or until chicken is no longer pink.

Serve chicken topped with corn salsa.

*Sodium is figured for reduced-salt.

Grilled Chicken with Fruit Salsa

Fruit Salsa
1 avocado, peeled, pitted and chopped
2 tablespoons lime juice
2 cups cubed fresh fruit such as red papaya,
    nectarine, apricot or peaches
4 green onions, chopped
1/2 cup chopped fresh cilantro
1/2 teaspoon chopped garlic
1/4 teaspoon salt (optional)
1/8 teaspoon ground black pepper

1 pound skinless, boneless chicken breasts,
    cut into strips
1/4 teaspoon salt (optional)
1/8 teaspoon ground
    black pepper

Pour lime juice over avocado to prevent browning. Mix with remaining salsa ingredients and set aside. Serve over cooked chicken.

Barbecue: When barbecue is hot, place chicken on grill. Season with salt and pepper. Cook about 4 minutes on each side or until chicken is no longer pink.

Conventional Oven: Preheat oven to 350 degrees. Place chicken in a 9-inch by 9-inch baking pan that has been sprayed with non-stick cooking spray. Season with salt and pepper. Bake for 20-30 minutes or until chicken is no longer pink.

Note: One serving is an excellent source of fiber.
Most of the fat in this recipe is heart-healthy monosaturated fat.

The fresh fruit salsa adds a unique taste to chicken. The barbecue method is the best but you can also prepare the chicken in your oven.

Makes 4 servings

Each Serving

Carb Servings*
1/2

Exchanges*
1/2 fruit
3 1/2 very lean meat
1 fat

Nutrient Analysis
calories 230
total fat 8g
saturated fat 1mg
cholesterol 65mg
sodium 84mg
total carbohydrate 13g
dietary fiber 5g
sugars 5g
protein 27g

*reflects carbohydrate
  minus fiber

This is best barbecued but can be broiled or baked. The hickory-flavored liquid smoke gives this dish an excellent flavor.

Makes 4 servings

Each Serving

Carb Servings
0

Exchanges
3 1/2 very lean meat

Nutrient Analysis
calories 127
total fat 1g
saturated fat 0mg
cholesterol 65mg
sodium 228mg
total carbohydrate 0g
dietary fiber 0g
sugars 0g
protein 26g

Hickory Smoked Barbecued Chicken

**1 pound skinless, boneless chicken breasts or
   2 pounds chicken parts
1/4 cup fat-free chicken broth,* or white wine
2 tablespoons lite soy sauce
2 tablespoons water
1 teaspoon liquid smoke
1/2 teaspoon ground ginger**

Skin chicken if parts are used.

Mix the remaining ingredients. Add chicken and marinate in the refrigerator for 1-3 hours. Drain marinade before cooking.

Barbecue: When barbecue is hot, place chicken on grill. Cook about 4 minutes on each side or until chicken is no longer pink.

Broil: Preheat oven to broil. Place chicken on broiler pan that has been sprayed with non-stick cooking spray. Cook about 4 minutes on each side or until chicken is no longer pink.

Conventional Oven: Preheat oven to 350 degrees. Place chicken in a 9-inch by 13-inch baking pan that has been sprayed with non-stick cooking spray. Bake for 20-30 minutes or until chicken is no longer pink.

*Sodium is figured for reduced-salt.

Chicken and Pea Pod Stir-Fry

1 pound skinless, boneless chicken breasts
1/2 cup cold water
2 tablespoons dry sherry or water (optional)
1 1/2 tablespoons lite soy sauce
1 tablespoon cornstarch
1 tablespoon chopped garlic
3 carrots, sliced diagonally
2 cups fresh snow pea pods
4 green onions, sliced

Cut chicken into bite-size pieces. Set aside.

In a small bowl combine water, sherry, soy sauce, cornstarch, and garlic. Set aside.

Spray a large skillet with non-stick cooking spray. Stir-fry chicken until no longer pink. Set aside and keep warm.

Add carrots to skillet and stir-fry for 3-5 minutes, adding water or broth, as needed, to prevent sticking. Add pea pods and onions. Stir-fry 2 minutes or until vegetables are crisp tender. Remove vegetables and keep warm.

Pour cornstarch mixture into skillet and stir until thickened and bubbly. Add vegetables and chicken. Cover and cook 1 minute.

Note: One serving is a good source of fiber.

This recipe has a light cornstarch gravy. It is especially good if you stir-fry the vegetables so that they are still crisp. Fresh broccoli can be substituted for the fresh pea pods.

Makes 4 servings

Each Serving

Carb Servings
1

Exchanges
3 vegetable
3 very lean meat

Nutrient Analysis
calories 188
total fat 2g
saturated fat 0mg
cholesterol 65mg
sodium 344mg
total carbohydrate 14g
dietary fiber 4g
sugars 5g
protein 28g

Fresh cilantro and fresh ginger are especially good in this recipe. Ground fresh chili paste can be found in the Asian foods section of the grocery store.

Makes 5 cups
5 servings

Each Serving
1 cup

Carb Servings
1

Exchanges
3/4 fruit
1 vegetable
3 very lean meat

Nutrient Analysis
calories 172 - with
   artificial sweetener 162
total fat 1g
saturated fat 0mg
cholesterol 52mg
sodium 383mg
total carbohydrate 17g - with
   artificial sweetener 15g
dietary fiber 2g
sugars 11g - with
   artificial sweetener 9g
protein 23g

Spicy Chicken and Grapes

1 tablespoon cornstarch
3/4 cup fat-free chicken broth,* divided
2 tablespoons lite soy sauce
1 tablespoon granulated sugar or the equivalent
   in artificial sweetener
1 tablespoon red wine vinegar
1 - 2 teaspoons ground fresh chili paste
1 pound skinless, boneless chicken breasts, cut
   into bite-size pieces
3 tablespoons fresh minced ginger
1 tablespoon chopped garlic
2 cups broccoli florets
1 1/2 cups green seedless grapes
3/4 cup green onions, thinly sliced
1/4 - 1/2 cup fresh cilantro (optional)

In a small bowl, combine cornstarch and 1/4 cup chicken broth. Add soy sauce, sugar, vinegar and chili paste. Set aside.

Spray a skillet with non-stick cooking spray. Add chicken, ginger and garlic. Stir-fry until chicken is no longer pink. Remove from skillet and keep warm.

Add broccoli to skillet and stir-fry until crisp tender, adding water or broth, as needed, to prevent sticking. Add grapes, green onions and the sauce mixture to the skillet.

Bring to a boil, stirring constantly for 1-2 minutes or until thickened. Mix in cooked chicken.

Top with cilantro just before serving.

*Sodium is figured for reduced-salt.

Sweet and Sour Chicken

1 can (8 ounces) unsweetened pineapple chunks,
   packed in juice
1 pound skinless, boneless chicken breasts
1 cup fat-free chicken broth*
1/4 cup cider vinegar
1/4 cup brown sugar or the equivalent in
   artificial sweetener**
2 teaspoons lite soy sauce
1/2 teaspoon chopped garlic
1 cup sliced celery
1 medium green pepper, sliced
1 small onion, quartered
3 tablespoons cornstarch
1/4 cup water

Drain pineapple, reserving the juice.

Cut chicken into bite-size pieces and place in a medium saucepan. Add reserved pineapple juice, broth, vinegar, brown sugar, soy sauce and garlic.

Cover and simmer over low heat for 15 minutes.

Add vegetables and pineapple. Cook 10 minutes, stirring occasionally.

Combine cornstarch and water. Gradually stir into hot mixture. Continue to cook until thickened, stirring constantly.

Serve with brown rice.

*Sodium is figured for reduced-salt.
**If using artificial sweetener, add after mixture is thickened with cornstarch.

This recipe will be enjoyed by all family members. Serve over brown rice or noodles.

Makes 5 cups
5 servings

Each Serving
1 cup

Carb Servings
1 1/2 - with
   artificial sweetener 1

Exchanges
1 fruit - 1/2 with
   artificial sweetener
1 vegetable
3 very lean meat

Nutrient Analysis
calories 193 - with
   artificial sweetener 152
total fat 1g
saturated fat 0mg
cholesterol 52mg
sodium 239mg
total carbohydrate 23g - with
   artificial sweetener 12g
dietary fiber 2g
sugars 16g - with
   artificial sweetener 5g
protein 22g

Makes 4 cups
4 servings

Each Serving
1 cup

Carb Servings
1

Exchanges
1/3 fruit
2 vegetable
3 1/2 very lean meat

Nutrient Analysis
calories 187
total fat 2g
saturated fat 0mg
cholesterol 65mg
sodium 297mg
total carbohydrate 15g
dietary fiber 3g
sugars 7g
protein 28g

Mandarin Orange Chicken

1 pound skinless, boneless chicken breasts, cut into strips
1 tablespoon minced fresh ginger
1-2 tablespoons lite soy sauce (optional)
2 cups red bell pepper strips
1 cup green onions, sliced in 1-inch pieces
3/4 cup fat-free chicken broth*
1 tablespoon cornstarch
1 can (11 ounces) mandarin oranges, drained
1 can (8 ounces) sliced water chestnuts, drained
hot cooked brown rice or noodles (optional)

Spray a large skillet with non-stick cooking spray. Add chicken, ginger and soy sauce. Stir-fry for 5-6 minutes or until chicken is no longer pink. Remove from skillet and keep warm.

Add red pepper and green onions to skillet. Stir-fry until crisp tender, adding water or broth, as needed, to prevent sticking.

In a small bowl, mix cornstarch with chicken broth. Stir into skillet. Cook, stirring constantly, until thickened.

Gently stir in cooked chicken, mandarin oranges and water chestnuts. Heat thoroughly.

Serve over brown rice or noodles.

If you are not on a sodium-restricted diet, serve with additional soy sauce.

*Sodium is figured for reduced-salt.

Note: One serving is a good source of fiber.

Chicken Cacciatore

1 1/2 pounds skinless, boneless chicken breasts or
** 2 1/2 pounds-3 pounds chicken parts**
1 can (14 ounces) stewed tomatoes*
1 can (8 ounces) tomato sauce*
1 medium onion, sliced
1 teaspoon Italian seasoning
2 cups frozen peas

Skin chicken if parts are used.

Spray a large saucepan with non-stick cooking spray.

Add chicken and remaining ingredients, except peas. Cover and simmer, stirring occasionally, for 25-35 minutes.

Add peas and cook for 10 minutes.

If adding dumplings, add 10 minutes before the peas. After adding the peas, cover and cook an additional 10 minutes.

*Sodium is figured for reduced-salt.

Note: One serving is a good source of fiber.

Variation: Canned green beans can be substituted for peas. Add during the last 5 minutes of cooking.

This has a delicious flavor and it is especially good when served with the Dumpling recipe in this book.

Makes 6 servings

Each Serving

Carb Servings
1

Exchanges
1/2 starch
1 vegetable
3 1/2 very lean meat

Nutrient Analysis
calories 179
total fat 2g
saturated fat 0mg
cholesterol 66mg
sodium 120mg
total carbohydrate 12g
dietary fiber 3g
sugars 6g
protein 28g

This is a great Oriental stir-fry dish that is colorful and delicious. It is pictured on the cover of this book.

Makes 6 cups
4 servings

Each Serving
1 1/2 cups

Carb Servings
1/2

Exchanges
2 vegetable
3 1/2 very lean meat
1 fat

Nutrient Analysis
calories 210
total fat 6g
saturated fat 1mg
cholesterol 65mg
sodium 427mg
total carbohydrate 10g
dietary fiber 3g
sugars 4g
protein 30g

Teriyaki Chicken Stir-Fry

1 pound skinless, boneless chicken breasts, cut in bite-size pieces
1/4 cup teriyaki sauce
2 teaspoons chopped garlic
1 cup sliced red bell pepper
1 cup sliced green bell pepper
8 green onions, cut in 1-inch pieces
1/3 cup dry roasted peanuts, unsalted

Combine chicken with teriyaki sauce and marinate for 1 hour in the refrigerator. Drain and discard marinade.

Spray a large skillet with non-stick cooking spray.

Stir-fry chicken with garlic until chicken is no longer pink. Remove chicken from skillet and keep warm.

Add peppers and onion to skillet. Stir-fry a few minutes or until vegetables are crisp-tender, adding water as needed to prevent sticking. Add chicken and peanuts.

Serve over rice or noodles.

Note: One serving is a good source of fiber.
Most of the fat in this recipe is heart-healthy monosaturated fat.

Seafood

It is far too easy to overcook fish. The general rule is to cook ten minutes for each inch of thickness. Fish should be cooked just until opaque and should flake easily with a fork.

The quality of frozen fish is usually very good as it is often frozen within four hours of being caught. Look for frozen cooked shrimp in place of canned. It has a better flavor and is lower in sodium.

This is best barbecued but can be broiled or baked. The hickory flavored liquid smoke gives this dish an excellent flavor.

Makes 4 servings

Each Serving

Carb Servings
0

Exchanges
3 lean meat

Nutrient Analysis
calories 164
total fat 7g
saturated fat 1mg
cholesterol 62mg
sodium 206mg
total carbohydrate 0g
dietary fiber 0g
sugars 0g
protein 23g

Hickory Smoked Barbecued Fish

1/4 cup fat-free chicken broth,* or white wine
2 tablespoons lite soy sauce
2 tablespoons water
1 teaspoon liquid smoke
1/2 teaspoon ground ginger
1 pound firm fish such as salmon, snapper or halibut

Mix the first five ingredients. Add fish and marinate in the refrigerator for 1-3 hours. Drain marinade before cooking.

Barbecue: Before starting barbecue, spray aluminum foil with non-stick cooking spray. **Note:** *Non-stick cooking spray is flammable. Do not spray near open flame or heated surfaces.* Place aluminum foil over rack, poking holes in several areas. Start barbecue. When hot, place fish on foil. Cook about 4 minutes on each side or until fish flakes easily.

Broil: Preheat oven to broil. Place fish on broiler pan that has been sprayed with non-stick cooking spray. Cook about 4 minutes on each side or until salmon flakes easily.

Oven Method: Preheat oven to 450 degrees. Arrange fish in a 9-inch by 13-inch baking pan that has been sprayed with non-stick cooking spray. Bake, uncovered, for 4-5 minutes per half inch thickness of fish. Drain any liquid.

*Sodium is figured for reduced-salt.

Grilled Salmon with Coconut-Cilantro Sauce

1 can (13 ounces) light coconut milk
4 sliced green onions
3 tablespoons minced fresh ginger
2 tablespoons lite soy sauce
2 tablespoons brown sugar or the equivalent
   in artificial sweetener
2 tablespoons fresh lime juice
2 teaspoons chopped garlic
1 teaspoon ground fresh chili paste
1 cup chopped fresh cilantro
2 pounds salmon fillets

In a small saucepan combine the first eight ingredients. Simmer for 5 minutes.

Barbecue: Before starting barbecue, spray aluminum foil with non-stick cooking spray. **Note:** *Non-stick cooking spray is flammable. Do not spray near open flame or heated surfaces.* Place foil over rack, poking holes in several areas. Start barbecue. When hot, place fish on foil. Spoon a couple tablespoons of coconut sauce over fish. Cook about 4 minutes on each side or until salmon flakes easily.

Oven Method: Preheat oven to 450 degrees. Arrange fish in a 9-inch by 13-inch baking pan that has been sprayed with non-stick cooking spray. Spoon a couple tablespoons of coconut sauce over fish. Bake for 4-5 minutes per half inch thickness of fish. Drain any liquid.

Add fresh cilantro to the sauce just before serving. Serve salmon with warm coconut-cilantro sauce.

Note: Most of the fat in this recipe is heart-healthy omega-3 fat.

The flavor of the coconut milk combined with fresh ginger and cilantro makes this Asian dish especially delicious. Light coconut milk has 60% less calories and fat than regular coconut milk.

Makes 8 servings

Each Serving

Carb Servings
1/2 - with
   artificial sweetener 0

Exchanges
1 vegetable
3 lean meat

Nutrient Analysis
calories 215 - with
   artificial sweetener 202
total fat 10g
saturated fat 4mg
cholesterol 62mg
sodium 224mg
total carbohydrate 7g - with
   artificial sweetener 3g
dietary fiber 0g
sugars 4g - with
   artificial sweetener 1g
protein 24g

This is a great recipe for a summer barbecue but can also be prepared in the oven. This salsa is especially flavorful.

Makes 8 servings

Each Serving

Carb Servings
1/2

Exchanges
1 vegetable
3 lean meat

Nutrient Analysis
calories 192
total fat 8g
saturated fat 1mg
cholesterol 62mg
sodium 62mg
total carbohydrate 7g
dietary fiber 1g
sugars 4g
protein 24g

Grilled Salmon with Corn Salsa

Corn Salsa
1 can (14 ounces) stewed tomatoes* or
   1 1/2 cups chopped fresh tomato
1 can (8 ounces) whole kernel corn,* drained
1 cup chopped cucumber, not peeled
1/2 cup chopped bell pepper, red or green
1/4 cup chopped fresh cilantro
2 tablespoons red wine vinegar
1/2 teaspoon each: garlic powder and ground cumin
1/4 teaspoon salt (optional)
1/8 teaspoon ground black pepper
1/8 teaspoon cayenne pepper

2 pounds salmon fillets
1/4 teaspoon salt (optional)
1/8 teaspoon ground black pepper

Combine salsa ingredients and set aside. Serve over cooked fish.

Barbecue: Before starting barbecue, spray aluminum foil with non-stick cooking spray. **Note:** *Non-stick cooking spray is flammable. Do not spray near open flame or heated surfaces.* Place aluminum foil over rack, poking holes in several areas. Start barbecue. When hot, place fish on foil. Season with salt and pepper. Cook about 4 minutes on each side or until salmon flakes easily.

Oven Method: Preheat oven to 450 degrees. Arrange fish in a 9-inch by 13-inch baking pan that has been sprayed with non-stick cooking spray. Season with salt and pepper. Bake, uncovered, for 4-5 minutes per half inch thickness of fish. Drain any liquid.

*Sodium is figured for reduced-salt.

Note: Most of the fat in this recipe is heart-healthy omega-3 fat.

Grilled Salmon with Fruit Salsa

Fruit Salsa
1 avocado, peeled, pitted and chopped
2 tablespoons lime juice
2 cups cubed fresh fruit such as red papaya,
   nectarine, apricot or peaches
2 green onions, chopped
1/4 cup chopped fresh cilantro
1/2 teaspoon chopped garlic
1/4 teaspoon salt (optional)
1/8 teaspoon ground black pepper

1 pound salmon fillets
1/4 teaspoon salt (optional)
1/8 teaspoon ground black pepper

Combine salsa ingredients and set aside. Serve over cooked fish.

Barbecue: Before starting barbecue, spray aluminum foil with non-stick cooking spray. **Note:** *Non-stick cooking spray is flammable. Do not spray near open flame or heated surfaces.* Place aluminum foil over rack, poking holes in several areas. Start barbecue. When hot, place fish on foil. Season with salt and pepper. Cook about 4 minutes on each side or until salmon flakes easily.

Conventional Oven: Preheat oven to 450 degrees. Arrange fish in a 9-inch by 13-inch baking pan that has been sprayed with non-stick cooking spray. Season with salt and pepper. Bake, uncovered, for 4-5 minutes per half inch thickness of fish. Drain any liquid.

Note: One serving is an excellent source of fiber.
Most of the fat in this recipe is heart-healthy monosaturated and omega-3 fat.

The fresh fruit salsa adds a unique taste to salmon. You can prepare the fish in your oven. However, the barbecue method is the best.

Makes 4 servings

Each Serving

Carb Servings*
1/2

Exchanges*
1/2 fruit
3 lean meat
1 fat

Nutrient Analysis
calories 264
total fat 14g
saturated fat 2mg
cholesterol 62mg
sodium 59mg
total carbohydrate 12g
dietary fiber 5g
sugars 5g
protein 24g

*reflects carbohydrate
 minus fiber

The liquid smoke gives an excellent flavor to this recipe. The marinade becomes a delicious sauce that is especially good served over rice or noodles.

Makes 4 servings

Each Serving

Carb Servings
1 - with
  artificial sweetener 0

Exchanges
1 starch - 0 with
  artificial sweetener
3 lean meat

Nutrient Analysis
calories 223 - with
  artificial sweetener 171
total fat 7g
saturated fat 1mg
cholesterol 62mg
sodium 367mg
total carbohydrate 14g - with
  artificial sweetener 1g
dietary fiber 0g
sugars 13g - with
  artificial sweetener 0g
protein 23g

Polynesian Fish

1/4 cup fat-free chicken broth,* or white wine
2 tablespoons lite soy sauce
2 tablespoons water
1 teaspoon liquid smoke
1/2 teaspoon ground ginger
1 pound of firm fish such as salmon or snapper
1/4 cup brown sugar or the equivalent in
  artificial sweetener
1 teaspoon ground mustard

Mix the first five ingredients. Add fish and marinate in the refrigerator for 1-3 hours.

Preheat oven to 450 degrees.

Add fish and the marinade to a 9-inch by 13-inch baking pan that has been sprayed with non-stick cooking spray.

Top fish pieces with 1/4 cup brown sugar and mustard.

Bake, uncovered, for 4-5 minutes per half inch thickness of fish.

Pour sauce over fish when serving.

*Sodium is figured for reduced-salt.

Salmon Cakes

1 can (15 ounces) red salmon, drained (or 2 cups flaked)
6 saltines (unsalted top), crushed
1/4 cup diced red pepper OR 1 can (2 ounces) canned pimento
3 tablespoons Miracle Whip Light
1 teaspoon onion powder
1 teaspoon lemon juice
4 drops Tabasco sauce

Remove skin from fish and mash salmon bones with a fork, if using canned. Add saltines and red pepper.

Combine remaining ingredients. Add to salmon and mix well.

Shape into 4 cakes.

Spray a skillet with non-stick cooking spray. Heat on medium.

Cook salmon cakes, turning once, until lightly browned on each side.

Note: Most of the fat in this recipe is heart-healthy omega-3 fat.

Cooking tip: Miracle Whip is preferred over mayonnaise as it adds a touch of sweetness.

This recipe is especially good with fresh red pepper but a jar of pimentos will do. Leftover salmon is good to use and it is much lower in sodium than the canned red salmon.

Makes 4 servings

Each Serving
1 cake

Carb Servings
1/2

Exchanges
1/2 starch
2 1/2 lean meat

Nutrient Analysis
calories 181
total fat 9g
saturated fat 2mg
cholesterol 40mg
sodium 496mg
total carbohydrate 6g
dietary fiber 0g
sugars 2g
protein 18g

Oven Fried Fish

1/4 cup cornflake crumbs
1/2 teaspoon Italian seasoning
1/8 teaspoon salt (optional)
1/8 teaspoon ground black pepper
1 pound fish fillets (such as snapper, sole, halibut)

Preheat oven to 450 degrees.

Spray a baking sheet with non-stick cooking spray. Mix the first four ingredients in a plastic bag and set aside.

Cut fish into serving size pieces. Place a few pieces of fish at a time in the plastic bag and shake to coat evenly.

Arrange on baking sheet so that fish is not touching. Bake for 10 minutes, per inch of thickness, or until fish flakes easily.

Oven Fried Oysters

1/2 cup cornflake crumbs
1 teaspoon Italian seasoning
1/4 teaspoon salt (optional)
1/8 teaspoon ground black pepper
1 jar (16 ounces) oysters, drained

Preheat oven to 425 degrees.

Spray a baking sheet with non-stick cooking spray.

Mix the first four ingredients in a plastic bag. Place oysters in the bag, a few at a time, and shake to coat. Arrange on baking sheet so oysters are not touching.

Bake for 10-15 minutes, depending on the size of the oysters.

Lemon Fish

This has a very good flavor and is so easy to prepare.

1 pound fish fillets (snapper, sole)
4-6 lemon slices
1/4 cup fat-free chicken broth* or white wine
1/2 teaspoon fat-free butter flavored sprinkles
1/8 teaspoon ground black pepper
1 tablespoon dried parsley

Arrange fish in a 9-inch by 13-inch baking pan that has been sprayed with non-stick cooking spray. Use a microwave-safe dish if cooking in the microwave.

Top with remaining ingredients.

Follow directions below for microwave or conventional oven.

Microwave Oven: Cover with plastic wrap, venting one corner. Cook on high for 5-8 minutes (depending on thickness), rotating 1/4 turn halfway through cooking. Fish is done when it flakes easily with a fork.

Conventional Oven: Preheat oven to 450 degrees. Bake fish, uncovered, for 10 minutes per inch of thickness, or until fish flakes easily with a fork.

*Sodium is figured for reduced salt.

Makes 4 servings

Each Serving

Carb Servings
0

Exchanges
3 very lean meat

Nutrient Analysis
calories 116
total fat 2g
saturated fat 0mg
cholesterol 42mg
sodium 120mg
total carbohydrate 1g
dietary fiber 0g
sugars 0g
protein 23g

The orange glaze adds color as well as flavor to the fish. This same glaze is used in French Glazed Chicken.

Makes 4 servings

Each Serving

Carb Servings
1/2

Exchanges
1/2 fruit
3 very lean meat

Nutrient Analysis
calories 145
total fat 2g
saturated fat 0mg
cholesterol 42mg
sodium 223mg
total carbohydrate 9g
dietary fiber 0g
sugars 3g
protein 23g

French Glazed Fish

1/4 cup nonfat French dressing
2 tablespoons sugar-free apricot preserves
2 tablespoons water
1 tablespoon dried or 1/4 cup fresh minced onion
1 pound fish fillets (snapper, sole)

Mix the first four ingredients and set aside.

Arrange fish in a 9-inch by 13-inch baking pan that has been sprayed with non-stick cooking spray. Use a microwave-safe dish if cooking in the microwave.

Follow directions below for microwave or conventional oven.

Conventional Oven: Preheat oven to 450 degrees. Bake, uncovered, for 4-5 minutes per 1/2 inch thickness of fish. Drain any liquid. Spoon apricot mixture over fish. Return to oven for 2 minutes to heat sauce.

Microwave Oven: Cover with plastic wrap, venting one corner. Cook on high for 4-6 minutes, depending on thickness of fish. Rotate 1/4 turn halfway through cooking time. Drain any liquid. Spoon apricot mixture over fish. Cook for 1-2 minutes or until sauce is heated.

Fish in Salsa

1 pound fish fillets (snapper, sole)
3/4 cup salsa

Arrange fish in a 9-inch by 13-inch baking pan that has been sprayed with non-stick cooking spray. Use a microwave-safe dish if cooking in the microwave.

Follow directions below for microwave or conventional oven.

Conventional Oven: Preheat oven to 450 degrees. Bake, uncovered, for 4-6 minutes per 1/2 inch thickness. Drain any liquid. Spoon salsa over fish. Return to oven for 2 minutes to heat salsa.

Microwave Oven: Cover with plastic wrap, venting one corner. Cook on high for 4-6 minutes, depending on thickness of fish. Rotate 1/4 turn halfway through cooking. Drain any liquid. Spoon salsa over fish. Cook for 1-2 minutes or until salsa is heated.

This is a favorite for salsa lovers. Sodium is figured for bottled salsa. To reduce the sodium, use the salsa recipe in this book.

Makes 4 servings

Each Serving

Carb Servings
0

Exchanges
1 vegetable
3 very lean meat

Nutrient Analysis
calories 128
total fat 2g
saturated fat 0mg
cholesterol 42mg
sodium 293mg
total carbohydrate 3g
dietary fiber 0g
sugars 2g
protein 23g

Makes 4 servings

Each Serving

Carb Servings
1/2

Exchanges
1 vegetable
3 very lean meat

Nutrient Analysis
calories 137
total fat 2g
saturated fat 0mg
cholesterol 43mg
sodium 88mg
total carbohydrate 6g
dietary fiber 1g
sugars 3g
protein 24g

Makes 4 servings

Each Serving

Carb Servings
0

Exchanges
3 very lean meat

Nutrient Analysis
calories 120
total fat 2g
saturated fat 0mg
cholesterol 42mg
sodium 169mg
total carbohydrate 1g
dietary fiber 0g
sugars 0g
protein 24g

Spanish Baked Fish

1 pound fish fillets (snapper or sole)
1 can (8 ounces) tomato sauce*
1/2 cup sliced onions
1/2 teaspoon each: chopped garlic and chili powder
1/4 teaspoon each: dried oregano and ground cumin

Preheat oven to 450 degrees.

Arrange fish in a 9-inch by 13-inch baking pan that has been sprayed with non-stick cooking spray.

Mix remaining ingredients and pour over fish. Bake for 10-20 minutes or until fish flakes easily.

*Sodium is figured for reduced-salt.

Poached Fish

1 cup fat-free chicken broth*
2 tablespoons lemon juice
1/2 teaspoon chopped garlic
1/4 teaspoon ground black pepper
2 bay leaves
2 tablespoons dry sherry (optional)
1 pound fish fillets (snapper, sole)

In a large skillet that has been sprayed with non-stick cooking spray, mix everything except fish. Bring to a boil. Reduce heat and add fish. Simmer, covered, for 3-5 minutes or until fish flakes easily.

Remove fish with slotted spatula. Discard bay leaves before serving.

*Sodium is figured for reduced-salt.

Sweet Mustard Fish

1 pound fish fillets (snapper, sole)
1/2 cup salsa, thick and chunky
2 tablespoons honey or the equivalent
**   in artificial sweetener***
2 tablespoons Dijon mustard

Arrange fish in a 9-inch by 13-inch baking pan that has been sprayed with non-stick cooking spray. Use a microwave-safe dish if cooking in the microwave.

Follow directions below for microwave or conventional oven.

Conventional Oven: Preheat oven to 450 degrees. Bake, uncovered, for 4-6 minutes per 1/2 inch thickness of fish. Drain any liquid. Combine remaining ingredients and spoon over fish. Return to oven for 2 minutes to heat sauce.

Microwave Oven: Cover with plastic wrap, venting one corner. Cook on high for 4-6 minutes, depending on thickness of fish. Rotate 1/4 turn halfway through cooking. Drain any liquid. Mix remaining ingredients and pour over fish. Cook for 1-2 minutes or until sauce is heated.

* Substitute 2 tablespoons of honey with 2-3 packets of Equal

This sauce adds an interesting taste. Sodium is figured for bottled salsa. To reduce the sodium, prepare the salsa recipe in this book.

Makes 4 servings

Each Serving

Carb Servings
1/2 - with
   artificial sweetener 0

Exchanges
1/2 starch - 0 with
   artificial sweetener
1/2 vegetable
3 very lean meat

Nutrient Analysis
calories 162 - with
   artificial sweetener 131
total fat 2g
saturated fat 0mg
cholesterol 42mg
sodium 400mg
total carbohydrate 10g - with
   artificial sweetener 2g
dietary fiber 0g
sugars 10g - with
   artificial sweetener 1g
protein 23g

This recipe has a distinct tarragon flavor that is good with fish.

Tarragon Fish

1 pound fish fillets (snapper, sole)
1/2 cup nonfat plain yogurt
1 teaspoon dried tarragon
1/4 cup (1 ounce) grated, reduced-fat
   mozzarella cheese

Arrange fish in a 9-inch by 13-inch baking pan that has been sprayed with non-stick cooking spray. Use a microwave-safe dish if cooking in the microwave.

Follow directions below for microwave or conventional oven.

Conventional Oven: Preheat oven to 450 degrees. Bake, uncovered, for 4-6 minutes per 1/2 inch thickness of fish. Drain any liquid. Mix remaining ingredients and spread over fish. Bake 2 minutes or until cheese is melted.

Microwave Oven: Cover with plastic wrap, venting one corner. Cook on high for 4-6 minutes, depending on thickness of fish. Rotate 1/4 turn halfway through cooking. Drain any liquid. Mix remaining ingredients and spread over fish. Cook for 1-2 minutes or until cheese is melted.

Makes 4 servings

Each Serving

Carb Servings
0

Exchanges
1/4 nonfat milk
3 very lean meat

Nutrient Analysis
calories 146
total fat 3g
saturated fat 1mg
cholesterol 47mg
sodium 139mg
total carbohydrate 2g
dietary fiber 0g
sugars 2g
protein 26g

Yogurt Cumin Fish

1 pound fish fillets (snapper, sole)
1/3 cup nonfat plain yogurt
3 tablespoons sugar-free apricot preserves
1 teaspoon ground cumin
1/2 teaspoon salt (optional)

Arrange fish in a 9-inch by 13-inch baking pan that has been sprayed with non-stick cooking spray. Use a microwave-safe dish if cooking in the microwave.

Follow directions below for microwave or conventional oven.

Conventional Oven: Preheat oven to 450 degrees. Bake, uncovered, for 4-5 minutes per 1/2 inch thickness of fish. Drain any liquid. Mix remaining ingredients and pour over fish. Bake for 2 minutes to heat sauce.

Microwave Oven: Cover with plastic wrap, venting one corner. Cook on high for 4-6 minutes, depending on thickness of fish. Rotate 1/4 turn halfway through cooking time. Drain any liquid. Mix remaining ingredients and pour over fish. Cook for 1-2 minutes or until sauce is heated.

This is a delicious way to serve fish when you're in a hurry. I like the combination of cumin with the sweetness of the apricot preserves.

Makes 4 servings

Each Serving

Carb Servings
0

Exchanges
1/3 fruit
3 very lean meat

Nutrient Analysis
calories 132
total fat 2g
saturated fat 0mg
cholesterol 42mg
sodium 88mg
total carbohydrate 5g
dietary fiber 0g
sugars 1g
protein 24g

Makes 8 servings

Each Serving

Carb Servings
0

Exchanges
3 1/2 very lean meat

Nutrient Analysis
calories 146
total fat 3g
saturated fat 1mg
cholesterol 46mg
sodium 137mg
total carbohydrate 3g
dietary fiber 0g
sugars 1g
protein 26g

Fillets of Sole Thermidor

2 pounds fillets of sole
1 teaspoon fat-free butter flavored sprinkles
3/4 cup nonfat milk, divided
2 tablespoons cornstarch
1/2 cup (2 ounces) grated, reduced-fat cheese
3 tablespoons dry sherry (optional)
dash of paprika

Preheat oven to 350 degrees.

Sprinkle fish fillets with butter flavored sprinkles.

Roll up each fillet. Place seam side down in a covered baking dish that has been sprayed with nonstick cooking spray. Pour 1/4 cup milk over fillets. Cover and bake for 25 minutes, or until fish flakes easily.

Meanwhile, mix 1/2 cup milk with cornstarch and microwave on high for 50 seconds, stirring once halfway through cooking (or cook in saucepan, stirring constantly until thickened).

Stir in cheese and sherry. Microwave for 20 seconds more (or continue to heat in saucepan).

Drain liquid from fish, discarding all but 1/2 cup. Add 1/2 cup of fish liquid to sauce. Pour over fish and sprinkle with paprika.

Variation: *Seafood Stuffed Fillets* - Fill each fillet with a tablespoon of shrimp or crab before rolling up. Also add 1/2 cup shrimp or crab to the sauce.

Mediterranean Seafood

6 ounces pasta of your choice
8 ounces fresh sliced mushrooms (about 3 cups)
2 red bell peppers, chopped (about 2 cups)
2 cups broccoli florets
1/2 cup sliced green onions
3 teaspoons chopped garlic
1 teaspoon Italian seasoning
1 teaspoon lemon pepper
1/2 teaspoon salt (optional)
1 pound scallops or shrimp (shelled and deveined)
1/2 cup fat-free chicken broth*
grated Parmesan cheese (optional)

Cook pasta according to package directions. Drain.

Meanwhile, spray a large skillet with non-stick cooking spray. Add seafood to skillet and cook until done. Remove from skillet and keep warm.

Add vegetables and seasonings to skillet. Stir-fry for about 4-5 minutes until crisp-tender. Add water or broth, as needed, to prevent sticking.

Add seafood, broth and hot noodles to vegetables. Toss well. Cover and let sit a couple of minutes before serving.

If desired, top with Parmesan cheese.

*Sodium is figured for reduced-salt.

Note: One serving is a good source of fiber.

Makes 9 cups
6 servings

Each Serving
1 1/2 cups

Carb Servings
2

Exchanges
1 1/2 starch
1 vegetable
2 very lean meat

Nutrient Analysis
calories 201
total fat 1g
saturated fat 0mg
cholesterol 25mg
sodium 163mg
total carbohydrate 28g
dietary fiber 3g
sugars 4g
protein 19g

This is a great warm weather dish. Serve as an hors d'oeuvre, sandwich or as a main dish. The optional toppings of peanuts and mint leaves add interest.

Makes 12 wraps
4 servings

Each Serving
3 wraps

Carb Servings
0

Exchanges
3 very lean meat

Nutrient Analysis
calories 129 - with
   artificial sweetener 121
total fat 1g
saturated fat 0mg
cholesterol 218mg
sodium 256mg
total carbohydrate 4g - with
   artificial sweetener 2g
dietary fiber 1g
sugars 3g - with
   artificial sweetener 1g
protein 24g

Shrimp Lettuce Wraps

1/4 cup rice vinegar
2 teaspoons sugar or the equivalent in
   artificial sweetener
1 pound cooked and cleaned salad shrimp
1/2 cup chopped green onion
1/4 cup chopped fresh cilantro
1/4 teaspoon crushed red pepper
1/4 teaspoon garlic powder
12 large lettuce leaves (bib or butter)

Optional Toppings:
mint leaves, chopped
dry roasted peanuts, coarsely chopped

In a medium bowl, mix rice vinegar and sugar. Stir to dissolve.

Add remaining ingredients, except the lettuce and optional toppings. If making in advance, add shrimp just before serving.

To serve, arrange bowl of shrimp, lettuce leaves and optional toppings on serving area.

To make each lettuce wrap, place about 1/4 cup of shrimp mixture in a lettuce leaf. Add optional toppings. Roll up and enjoy!

Variation: *Shrimp Pitas:* Cut 3 pocket breads in half. Line each with lettuce. Add 1/2 cup of shrimp mixture to each pocket.

Spicy Seafood and Grapes

1 tablespoon cornstarch
3/4 cup fat-free chicken broth,* divided
2 tablespoons lite soy sauce
1 tablespoon granulated sugar or the equivalent
   in artificial sweetener
1 tablespoon red wine vinegar
1 - 2 teaspoons ground fresh chili paste
1 pound scallops or cleaned shrimp
3 tablespoons fresh minced ginger
1 tablespoon chopped garlic
2 cups broccoli florets
1 1/2 cups green seedless grapes
3/4 cup green onions, thinly sliced
1/4 - 1/2 cup fresh cilantro (optional)

In a small bowl, combine cornstarch and 1/4 cup chicken broth. Add soy sauce, sugar, vinegar and chili paste.

Spray a skillet with non-stick cooking spray. Add seafood, ginger and garlic. Stir-fry until seafood is cooked. Remove from skillet and keep warm.

Add broccoli to skillet and stir-fry until crisp tender, adding water or broth, as needed, to prevent sticking. Add grapes, green onions and sauce mixture to the skillet.

Bring to a boil, stirring constantly for 1-2 minutes or until thickened. Mix in cooked seafood.

Top with cilantro just before serving.

*Sodium is figured for reduced-salt.

Fresh cilantro and fresh ginger are especially good in this recipe. The ground fresh chili paste can be found in the Asian foods section of your local grocery store.

Makes 5 cups
4 servings

Each Serving
1 1/4 cups

Carb Servings
1 1/2

Exchanges
1 fruit
1 vegetable
3 very lean meat

Nutrient Analysis
calories 192 - with
   artificial sweetener 179
total fat 1g
saturated fat 0mg
cholesterol 37mg
sodium 588mg
total carbohydrate 24g - with
   artificial sweetener 21g
dietary fiber 2g
sugars 14g - with
   artificial sweetener 11g
protein 22g

Makes 4 cups
4 servings

Each Serving
1 cup

Carb Servings
1

Exchanges
1/3 fruit
2 vegetable
3 very lean meat

Nutrient Analysis
calories 163
total fat 1g
saturated fat 0mg
cholesterol 37mg
sodium 407mg
total carbohydrate 17g
dietary fiber 3g
sugars 7g
protein 21g

Mandarin Orange Seafood

1 pound scallops or shrimp (shelled & deveined)
1 tablespoon minced fresh ginger
1-2 tablespoons lite soy sauce (optional)
1 cup green onions, sliced in 1-inch pieces
2 cups red bell pepper strips
1 tablespoon cornstarch
3/4 cup fat-free chicken broth*
1 can (11 ounces) mandarin oranges, drained
1 can (8 ounces) sliced water chestnuts, drained
hot cooked brown rice or noodles (optional)

Spray a large skillet with non-stick cooking spray. Add seafood, ginger and soy sauce. Stir-fry a few minutes or until seafood is done. Remove from skillet and keep warm.

Add green onions and red pepper to skillet. Stir-fry until crisp tender, adding water or broth, as needed, to prevent sticking.

In a small bowl, mix cornstarch with chicken broth. Stir into skillet. Cook, stirring constantly, until thickened.

Gently stir in cooked seafood, mandarin oranges and water chestnuts. Heat thoroughly.

Serve over brown rice or noodles.

*Sodium is figured for reduced-salt.

Note: One serving is a good source of fiber.

Clam Fettucini

12 ounces uncooked fettucini noodles (eggless)
3 cans (6 ounces each) minced clams,
not drained
1 tablespoon chopped garlic
1 tablespoon lemon juice
1/2 teaspoon dried thyme
1/4 teaspoon salt (optional)

Cook noodles according to package directions. Drain.

Return noodles to pan and add remaining ingredients.
Heat thoroughly. Turn off heat.

Cover and let sit until liquid is absorbed or if you prefer
more moisture, serve immediately.

*This recipe uses staple
foods that I keep stocked
in my cupboard. It's
quick to put together
and it has been one of
my children's favorite
dishes. Serve topped
with Parmesan cheese.*

Makes 7 cups
7 servings

Each Serving
1 cup

Carb Servings
2 1/2

Exchanges
2 1/2 starch
2 very lean meat

Nutrient Analysis
calories 273
total fat 2g
saturated fat 0mg
cholesterol 41mg
sodium 56mg
total carbohydrate 39g
dietary fiber 2g
sugars 2g
protein 23g

Lemon Basil Marinade

1/4 cup lemon juice
2 tablespoons olive oil
2 tablespoons finely chopped green onion
1/2 teaspoon dried basil or 1 tablespoon fresh
1/4 teaspoon salt (optional)

Mix all ingredients. Add fish and marinate for one to four hours in the refrigerator.

Drain marinade and broil or barbecue fish until done.

Note: This amount is enough to marinate 1-2 pounds of seafood. The nutrition information is for the approximate amount of marinade retained in a cooked three ounce portion of seafood.

Soy Marinade

1/4 cup oil (canola or olive)
1/4 cup white wine
3 tablespoons lite soy sauce
2 tablespoons water
1 teaspoon chopped garlic
1/2 teaspoon ground ginger

Mix marinade ingredients. Add fish and marinate for one to four hours in the refrigerator.

Drain marinade and barbecue or broil fish until done.

Note: This amount is enough to marinate 1-2 pounds of seafood. The nutrition information is for the approximate amount of marinade retained in a cooked three ounce portion of seafood.

Beef and Pork

Lean beef and pork are good choices. Choose cuts such as top sirloin or tenderloin and trim off all visible fat. Less marbling also means less fat. Broiling or barbecuing are good methods for cooking since the fat drips out.

Makes 4 servings

Each Serving

Carb Servings
0

Exchanges
1/3 starch
3 lean meat

Nutrient Analysis
calories 167
total fat 5g
saturated fat 2mg
cholesterol 62mg
sodium 91mg
total carbohydrate 5g
dietary fiber 0g
sugars 1g
protein 26g

Oven Fried Pork Loin

1/4 cup cornflake crumbs
1/4 teaspoon dried thyme
1/4 teaspoon dried sage
1/8 teaspoon salt (optional)
1/8 teaspoon ground black pepper
1 pound boneless top loin pork chops (about 3/4-inch to 1-inch thick), well trimmed

Preheat oven to 350 degrees.

Spray an 8-inch by 8-inch baking dish with non-stick cooking spray.

Mix the first five ingredients in a plastic bag. Place a couple pieces of pork in the plastic bag and shake to coat evenly.

Arrange pork in the baking pan so that they are not touching.

Bake for 20-25 minutes or until pork is cooked.

Variation: *Italian Oven Fried Pork* - Substitute 1/2 teaspoon of Italian seasoning for the sage and thyme.

Orange Pork Chops

1/3 cup sugar-free orange marmalade
2 tablespoons Dijon mustard
4 pork rib chops (cut 3 per pound)
3 - 4 bunches of green onions

In a small saucepan mix marmalade and mustard. Stir over medium heat until marmalade is melted. Set aside.

Trim all fat from chops. Place chops on rack of a broiler pan or use the outdoor barbecue.

Broil about 4 inches from the heat for 6 minutes. Turn chops and broil for 2 more minutes. Spoon half of the glaze over chops.

Broil 4-5 minutes more or until chops are cooked.

Meanwhile, slice onions diagonally into 1-inch pieces.

Spray a skillet with non-stick cooking spray. Add onions and stir-fry 2 minutes or until crisp-tender.

Stir in remaining glaze and heat thoroughly. Serve over chops.

This is a delicious and unusual way to serve pork chops. It is a good dish for entertaining, especially if you use the outdoor barbecue.

Makes 4 servings

Each Serving

Carb Servings
1/2

Exchanges
1/2 fruit
1 vegetable
3 lean meat

Nutrient Analysis
calories 210
total fat 7g
saturated fat 3mg
cholesterol 62mg
sodium 240mg
total carbohydrate 10g
dietary fiber 1g
sugars 1g
protein 26g

This casserole can be assembled in minutes. The combination of vegetables with rice and meat makes meal planning simple.

Makes 4 cups
4 servings

Each Serving
1 cup

Carb Servings
2

Exchanges
1 1/2 starch
1 vegetable
3 lean meat

Nutrient Analysis
calories 291
total fat 8g
saturated fat 2mg
cholesterol 64mg
sodium 569mg
total carbohydrate 27g
dietary fiber 3g
sugars 3g
protein 29g

Pork and Rice Casserole

1 cup uncooked quick-cooking brown rice
1 pound boneless pork top loin
1 cup chopped onion
1 cup sliced celery
1 can (10 ounces) reduced-fat cream of celery soup*
1/2 can water
1/2 teaspoon dried marjoram
1/2 teaspoon dried thyme
1/4 teaspoon salt (optional)
1/4 teaspoon ground black pepper

Preheat oven to 350 degrees.

Spray a covered 2-quart casserole with non-stick cooking spray. Spread rice in the casserole.

Cut pork into bite-size pieces. Brown pork in a skillet that has been sprayed with non-stick cooking spray.

Top rice with pork, onion and celery.

Mix seasonings and water with the soup. Pour over all.

Cover and bake for 45 minutes. Let sit ten minutes before serving.

*To reduce sodium, choose soups that are also 30% less sodium.

Note: One serving is a good source of fiber.

Chinese Pepper Steak

**1 pound boneless beef top sirloin, cut into
thin strips**
2 cups fat-free beef broth*
2 green peppers, sliced
1 1/2 cups diagonally sliced celery
1 cup sliced onion
1 teaspoon chopped garlic
1/2 teaspoon salt (optional)
1/2 teaspoon ground black pepper
**1/2 teaspoon sugar or the equivalent in
artificial sweetener**
1/4 cup cornstarch
2 teaspoons lite soy sauce
1/2 cup water

Spray a large skillet with non-stick cooking spray.

Add beef strips and stir-fry until browned.

Add all but the last three ingredients and simmer,
covered, for 4-8 minutes.

Meanwhile, in a small bowl, mix cornstarch with soy
sauce and water. Stir into hot mixture and continue
cooking, stirring constantly, until thickened.

Serve over noodles or quick-cooking brown rice.

*Sodium is figured for reduced-salt.

Note: One serving is a good
source of fiber.

*This is a family
favorite that tastes
great. If you like crisp
vegetables, simmer for
the lesser time.*

Makes 5 cups
4 servings

Each Serving
1 1/4 cups

Carb Servings
1

Exchanges
1/2 starch
2 vegetable
3 lean meat

Nutrient Analysis
calories 253 - with
artificial sweetener 251
total fat 9g
saturated fat 3mg
cholesterol 66mg
sodium 388mg
total carbohydrate 16g - with
artificial sweetener 16
dietary fiber 3g
sugars 4g
protein 26g

Pork Chop Suey

1 pound boneless pork tenderloin
2 cups sliced celery
1 cup sliced onion
1 cup fat-free beef broth*
1 tablespoon lite soy sauce
1/4 teaspoon salt (optional)
2 1/2 tablespoons cornstarch
1/4 cup water
1 tablespoon molasses
1/4 teaspoon ground ginger
1 can (16 ounces) bean sprouts,
drained (or fresh)

Cut pork into 1-inch strips, 1/4-inch thick.

Brown pork in a large skillet that has been sprayed with non-stick cooking spray.

Add the next five ingredients, cover and simmer for 5-10 minutes.

Meanwhile, in a small bowl, mix cornstarch, water, molasses and ginger. Stir into hot mixture and bring to a boil, stirring constantly until thickened.

Add bean sprouts and heat thoroughly.

Serve over noodles or quick-cooking brown rice.

*Sodium is figured for reduced-salt.

Using pork tenderloin eliminates the extra trimming of fat and bone. It also makes this a quick and tasty dish. If you like crisp vegetables, simmer for the lesser amount of time.

Makes 5 cups
4 servings

Each Serving
1 1/4 cups

Carb Servings
1

Exchanges
1/3 starch
2 vegetable
3 lean meat

Nutrient Analysis
calories 219
total fat 5g
saturated fat 2mg
cholesterol 62mg
sodium 366mg
total carbohydrate 16g
dietary fiber 2g
sugars 7g
protein 28g

Italian Pork Skillet*

1 pound boneless pork top loin, cut into strips
1/2 teaspoon chopped garlic
1 small eggplant, not peeled (about 12-14 ounces),
**   cut into one-inch cubes (about 4 cups)**
2 cups sliced summer squash
1 medium onion, sliced
1 medium red pepper, cut into strips
1 teaspoon Italian seasoning
1/2 teaspoon salt (optional)
1/4 teaspoon ground black pepper
1/2 cup water
1 1/2 teaspoons cornstarch

Spray a large skillet with non-stick cooking spray. Heat on medium and add pork and garlic to brown. Remove from skillet and keep warm.

Add the vegetables and seasonings to the skillet. Stir-fry a couple of minutes adding water or broth, as needed, to prevent sticking.

Add browned pork and cook until pork is no longer pink and vegetables are crisp-tender.

Combine water and cornstarch. Add to skillet and cook, stirring constantly, until thickened.

*Recipe adapted from National Pork Board.

Note: One serving is a good source of fiber.

This is such an easy dish. It is very flavorful and uses a variety of vegetables. You can easily vary this recipe by using different vegetables.

Makes 6 cups
4 servings

Each Serving
1 1/2 cups

Carb Servings
1

Exchanges
2 vegetable
3 lean meat

Nutrient Analysis
calories 198
total fat 5g
saturated fat 2mg
cholesterol 62mg
sodium 60mg
total carbohydrate 12g
dietary fiber 4g
sugars 5g
protein 28g

This is a quick dish that the entire family will enjoy.

Makes 4 servings

Each Serving

Carb Servings
2

Exchanges
1 2/3 starch
1 vegetable
3 lean meat

Nutrient Analysis
calories 332
total fat 10g
saturated fat 3mg
cholesterol 66mg
sodium 267mg
total carbohydrate 30g
dietary fiber 3g
sugars 6g
protein 29g

Beef or Pork Fajitas

1 pound boneless beef top sirloin or
   pork tenderloin
1 medium green bell pepper, sliced
1 medium onion, sliced
3 tablespoons lime juice
1/2 teaspoon coriander
1/2 teaspoon chili powder
4 (8-inch) or 8 (6-inch) whole wheat tortillas
salsa (optional)

Cut meat into 1-inch strips. In a medium bowl, combine meat and vegetables.

Mix lime juice with coriander and chili powder. Pour over meat and vegetables. Set aside for a few minutes or for up to one hour.

Spray a skillet with non-stick cooking spray.

Stir-fry meat and vegetables until done.

Warm tortillas in microwave about 50 seconds on high or in a non-stick skillet.

Fill each tortilla with meat mixture. Serve with salsa.

Note: One serving is a good source of fiber.

Fajitas Barbecue Style

Marinade:
1/3 cup lime juice
1 teaspoon dried oregano
1 teaspoon chili powder
1/2 teaspoon garlic powder
1/4 teaspoon salt (optional)
1/4 teaspoon ground black pepper

1 pound beef top sirloin steak, 1-inch thick
4 (8-inch) or 8 (6-inch) whole wheat tortillas
1 cup each: shredded lettuce and chopped tomato
1/2 cup sliced green onion

Mix marinade ingredients in a container large enough to hold the steak.

Add steak, coating both sides with the marinade. Refrigerate for 1 hour, turning halfway through marinating time. Drain marinade and discard.

Broil or barbecue steak about 2-3 minutes on each side or until desired doneness.

Carve crossgrain into thin slices.

Heat tortillas in microwave or in a non-stick skillet.

To serve, portion meat, lettuce, tomato and onions on tortillas.

Note: One serving is a good source of fiber.

This is a great barbecue dish that is so simple to prepare. It will be a family favorite.

Makes 4 servings

Each Serving

Carb Servings
1 1/2

Exchanges
1 1/2 starch
1 vegetable
3 lean meat

Nutrient Analysis
calories 328
total fat 10g
saturated fat 3mg
cholesterol 66mg
sodium 273mg
total carbohydrate 25g
dietary fiber 4g
sugars 5g
protein 29g

This is a favorite marinade for steaks. It really adds a good flavor.

Makes 6 servings

Each Serving

Carb Servings
0

Exchanges
3 lean meat

Nutrient Analysis
calories 185
total fat 9g
saturated fat 3mg
cholesterol 66mg
sodium 411mg
total carbohydrate 1g
dietary fiber 0g
sugars 0g
protein 24g

Marinated Steak

Marinade:
1/3 cup lite soy sauce
1/3 cup chili sauce
1/4 cup water
1 tablespoon Worcestershire sauce
1 tablespoon dried parsley
1 teaspoon dried oregano
1/4 teaspoon ground black pepper
1/4 teaspoon garlic powder
1/8 teaspoon chili powder
1/8 teaspoon ground mustard

1 1/2 pounds boneless steak (top sirloin, flank, or round), well trimmed

Mix marinade ingredients in a container large enough to hold the steak.

Add steak, coating both sides with the marinade. Refrigerate and marinate for 2 to 4 hours, turning steak once halfway through the marinating time. Drain marinade.

Broil or barbecue steak about 2-3 minutes on each side or until desired doneness.

Carve crossgrain into thin slices.

Pork or Beef Stir-Fry

1 pound lean pork top loin or top sirloin beef
1 teaspoon chopped garlic
2 cups fresh broccoli florets
1 cup sliced carrots
1 cup sliced red bell pepper
1 small zucchini, cut into strips
1 - 2 teaspoons lite soy sauce
1/4 teaspoon ground black pepper

Cut meat into strips 1/4-inch thick.

Spray a skillet with non-stick cooking spray. Add meat and stir-fry with garlic until browned. Remove and keep warm.

Stir-fry carrots until partially done. Add water or broth, as needed, to prevent sticking. Add remaining vegetables and stir-fry a few minutes.

Add meat, soy sauce and pepper. Continue to stir-fry until vegetables and meat are done to your liking.

Serve with rice or noodles.

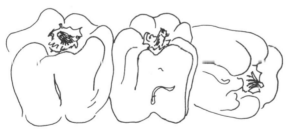

Cooking tip: Vegetables that work well in this recipe are green, yellow or orange bell peppers, celery, green onions, yellow onions, cauliflower, cabbage, snow peas, mushrooms and bean sprouts.

Note: One serving is a good source of fiber.

I use 4 to 5 cups of sliced vegetables in this recipe. If you use different vegetables each time you make this, it will seem like a new recipe. Tougher vegetables should be added first for longer cooking.

Makes 4 servings

Each Serving

Carb Servings
1/2

Exchanges
2 Vegetable
3 lean meat

Nutrient Analysis
calories 213
total fat 9g
saturated fat 3mg
cholesterol 66mg
sodium 145mg
total carbohydrate 8g
dietary fiber 3g
sugars 4g
protein 25g

Ground Meat Dishes

Ground beef, ground turkey or ground venison or elk may be used in any of the recipes in this section. When buying ground beef or turkey, look for 7% fat or less. If you have wild meat butchered, ask not to have fat added to the meat.

This Asian dish can be served wrapped in lettuce or in pita bread. Serve as an hors d'oeuvre, sandwich or as a main dish. The optional toppings of mint and peanuts make this dish unique.

Makes 12 wraps
4 servings

Each Serving
3 wraps

Carb Servings
0

Exchanges
1 vegetable
3 lean meat

Nutrient Analysis
calories 177
total fat 8g
saturated fat 3mg
cholesterol 70mg
sodium 108mg
total carbohydrate 4g
dietary fiber 1g
sugars 2g
protein 23g

Beef Lettuce Wraps

1 pound extra lean ground beef or ground turkey (7% fat)
1/2 cup sliced green onion
2 tablespoons minced fresh ginger
2 tablespoons orange juice
2 tablespoons lime juice
1/2 - 1 teaspoon ground fresh chili paste
1/4 teaspoon salt (optional)
1/2 cup chopped fresh cilantro
12 large lettuce leaves (bib or butter)

Optional Toppings:
mint leaves, chopped
dry roasted peanuts, coarsely chopped

In a medium saucepan, that has been sprayed with non-stick cooking spray, sauté meat with onion and ginger. Add orange juice, lime juice, chili paste and salt.

Simmer about 10 minutes or until meat is cooked. Add cilantro.

To serve, arrange bowl of meat mixture, lettuce leaves and optional toppings on serving area.

To make each lettuce wrap, place about 1/4 cup of meat mixture in a lettuce leaf. Add optional toppings. Roll up and enjoy!

Note: The ground fresh chili paste can be found in the Asian foods section of your local grocery store. Use the larger amount if you like spicy foods.

Variation: *Beef Pitas* - Cut 3 pocket breads in half. Line each with lettuce. Add 1/2 cup of meat mixture to each pocket. Makes 6 halves.

Turkey Lettuce Wraps

1 pound extra lean ground turkey (7% fat)
1/2 cup sliced green onion
2 tablespoons minced fresh ginger
1 can (8 ounces) water chestnuts, chopped
1 teaspoon sesame oil
1 teaspoon lite soy sauce
1/4 teaspoon salt (optional)
1/4 cup chopped fresh cilantro
12 large lettuce leaves (bib or butter)

Optional Toppings:
mint leaves, chopped
dry roasted peanuts,
coarsely chopped

In a medium saucepan, that has been sprayed with non-stick cooking spray, sauté turkey with onion and ginger. Add water chestnuts, oil, soy sauce and salt.

Continue to cook until meat is done. Add cilantro.

To serve, arrange bowl of meat mixture, lettuce leaves and optional toppings on serving area.

To make each lettuce wrap, place about 1/4 cup of meat mixture in a lettuce leaf. Add optional toppings. Roll up and enjoy!

Variation: *Turkey Pitas:* Cut 3 pocket breads in half. Line each with lettuce. Add 1/2 cup of meat mixture to each pocket. Makes 6 halves.

This Asian dish can be served wrapped in lettuce or in pita bread. Serve as an hors d'oeuvre, sandwich or as a main dish. The turkey provides a mild flavor and the chestnuts add a crunchy texture.

Makes 12 wraps
4 servings

Each Serving
3 wraps

Carb Servings
1/2

Exchanges
1 vegetable
3 lean meat

Nutrient Analysis
calories 185
total fat 8g
saturated fat 2mg
cholesterol 65mg
sodium 137mg
total carbohydrate 6g
dietary fiber 2g
sugars 1g
protein 23g

Makes 4 servings

Each Serving

Carb Servings
1/2

Exchanges
2/3 starch
3 lean meat

Nutrient Analysis
calories 224
total fat 9g
saturated fat 3mg
cholesterol 71mg
sodium 127mg
total carbohydrate 10g
dietary fiber 1g
sugars 2g
protein 26g

Meat Patties

1/2 cup oatmeal or oat bran
1/2 cup nonfat milk
1/4 cup egg substitute (equal to 1 egg)
1/2 tablespoon dried parsley
1 teaspoon ground mustard
1 teaspoon dried or 1 tablespoon fresh
    minced onion
1/2 teaspoon salt (optional)
1/4 teaspoon chopped garlic
1/4 teaspoon ground black pepper
1 pound extra lean ground beef or
    ground turkey (7% fat)

Mix the first nine ingredients. Add ground meat and mix well.

Shape into 6 patties.

Cook in the microwave, conventional oven or on the barbecue.

Conventional Oven: Preheat oven to 425 degrees. Arrange patties on a baking pan that has been sprayed with non-stick cooking spray. Bake for 20 minutes.

Microwave Oven: Arrange meat patties in a circle, on a microwave-safe dish, leaving the center empty. Cover with wax paper and cook on high for 7-8 minutes, rotating 1/4 turn halfway through cooking time.

Barbecue: Cook over hot coals, turning once, until done.

Baked Meatballs

1 cup oatmeal or oat bran
1 cup nonfat milk
1/2 cup egg substitute (equal to 2 eggs)
1 tablespoon dried parsley
2 teaspoons onion powder
1 teaspoon salt (optional)
1/2 teaspoon ground black pepper
1/4 teaspoon ground nutmeg
2 pounds extra lean ground beef or
**   ground turkey (7% fat)**

Preheat oven to 425 degrees.

Mix the first eight ingredients. Add ground meat and mix well.

Shape into 1 1/2-inch balls.

Arrange on baking sheets that have been sprayed with non-stick cooking spray.

Bake for 12 minutes or until done.

Baked Meatballs are used in the following recipes:
Swedish Meatballs, page 220
Spaghetti and Meatballs, page 220
Meatball Sandwich, page 129

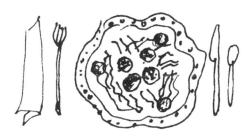

These are so quick because you cook them in the oven. Make this large amount and freeze for later use. These taste great in the recipes listed below.

Makes 48 meatballs
12 servings

Each Serving
4 meatballs

Carb Servings
1/2

Exchanges
1/2 starch
2 lean meat

Nutrient Analysis
calories 146
total fat 6g
saturated fat 2mg
cholesterol 47mg
sodium 85mg
total carbohydrate 6g
dietary fiber 1g
sugars 1g
protein 17g

Makes 6 servings

Each Serving

Carb Servings
2

Exchanges
1 1/4 starch
2 vegetable
2 lean meat

Nutrient Analysis
calories 277
total fat 9g
saturated fat 2mg
cholesterol 47mg
sodium 591mg
total carbohydrate 28g
dietary fiber 4g
sugars 8g
protein 21g

Spaghetti and Meatballs

24 meatballs (page 219)
1 jar (26 ounces) spaghetti sauce
   (less than 4 g fat per 4 ounces)
3 cups cooked spaghetti noodles

Heat meatballs in sauce. Serve over spaghetti noodles.

Note: One serving is a good source of fiber.

Cooking tip: This is quick to prepare if you have meatballs in the freezer and sauce in the cupboard.

Makes 4 servings

Each Serving

Carb Servings
1

Exchanges
2/3 starch
3 lean meat

Nutrient Analysis
calories 214
total fat 8g
saturated fat 3mg
cholesterol 59mg
sodium 264mg
total carbohydrate 13g
dietary fiber 2g
sugars 1g
protein 23g

Swedish Meatballs

20 meatballs (page 219)
1 can (14 ounces) fat-free beef or chicken broth*
3 1/2 tablespoons unbleached all-purpose flour

Pour 1/4 of the broth in a covered container. Add flour and shake well to prevent lumps.

In a saucepan, combine remainder of broth with the flour mixture. Bring to a boil, stirring constantly with a wire whisk, until thickened. Add meatballs and heat.

*Sodium is figured for reduced-salt.

Variation: *Swedish Meatballs and Mushrooms* - Add one small can of drained mushrooms to the gravy when adding the meatballs.

Asparagus Topped Meatloaf

1/2 cup oatmeal or oat bran
1/4 cup nonfat milk
1/4 cup egg substitute
   (equal to 1 egg)
1/2 tablespoon dried parsley
1/2 teaspoon salt (optional)
1/4 teaspoon ground black pepper
1 pound extra lean ground beef or
   ground turkey (7% fat)
3/4 pound asparagus spears, trimmed
   or 3 cups bite-size broccoli florets
1 can (13 ounces) mushroom pieces
   and stems, drained
1 can (10 ounces) reduced-fat cream
   of mushroom soup*
1/4 can water
1/2 teaspoon paprika
1/8 teaspoon ground black pepper

Preheat oven to 350 degrees.

Combine the first six ingredients. Add ground meat and mix well.

Press meat mixture in an 8-inch by 8-inch baking pan that has been sprayed with non-stick cooking spray.

If asparagus spears are very thick, cut in half, lengthwise. Arrange vegetables over meat.

Mix soup and water. Spread over vegetables. Sprinkle with paprika and pepper. Bake for 40 minutes or until asparagus is crisp-tender and meat is cooked.

*To reduce sodium, choose soups that are also 30% less sodium.

Note: One serving is a good source of fiber.

The canned soup in this recipe makes a nice gravy. Bite-size broccoli pieces can be substituted for the asparagus. When preparing asparagus, snap off the fibrous end and soak the tips in water to remove any dirt.

Makes 4 servings

Each Serving

Carb Servings
1

Exchanges
1 starch
1 vegetable
3 lean meat

Nutrient Analysis
calories 286
total fat 10g
saturated fat 4mg
cholesterol 73mg
sodium 469mg
total carbohydrate 19g
dietary fiber 4g
sugars 4g
protein 29g

This is a family favorite that can be put together in a hurry. Serve with a salad and a whole grain roll.

Makes 4 servings

_____

Each Serving

Carb Servings
0

Exchanges
1/2 vegetable
3 lean meat

Nutrient Analysis
calories 187
total fat 9g
saturated fat 4mg
cholesterol 74mg
sodium 183mg
total carbohydrate 2g
dietary fiber 0g
sugars 1g
protein 24g

Pizza Meat Loaf

**1 pound extra lean ground beef or
   ground turkey (7% fat)
1/4 cup pizza sauce
1/4 cup (1 ounce) grated, reduced-fat
   mozzarella cheese
1/2 cup thin sliced vegetables such as
   green pepper and onion**

Spray a 9-inch glass pie plate with non-stick cooking spray. Pack the meat lightly onto the pie plate.

Follow the directions below for microwave or conventional oven.

Conventional Oven: Preheat oven to 425 degrees. Bake for 12-14 minutes. Drain any liquid. Top with pizza sauce, cheese and vegetables. Return to oven for 5 minutes.

Microwave Oven: Cover with wax paper and cook on high for 6 minutes, turning 1/4 turn halfway through cooking time. Drain any liquid. Top with pizza sauce, cheese and vegetables. Cook on high for 2 minutes until cheese is melted.

Meat Loaf

3/4 cup oatmeal
3/4 cup nonfat milk
1/2 cup catsup
1/4 cup egg substitute (equal to 1 egg)
1 tablespoon dried parsley
1 teaspoon ground mustard
1 teaspoon salt (optional)
1/2 teaspoon chopped garlic
1/2 teaspoon ground black pepper
1/2 cup finely chopped onion
1/2 cup finely chopped green pepper or celery
1 1/2 pounds extra lean ground beef or ground
    turkey (7% fat)

Mix the first nine ingredients. Add vegetables and ground meat. Mix well.

Follow the directions below for microwave or conventional oven.

Conventional Oven: Preheat oven to 325 degrees. Pack meat mixture in a loaf pan that has been sprayed with non-stick cooking spray. Bake for 1 hour.

Microwave Oven: Pack meat mixture lightly into a 10-inch glass dish that has been sprayed with non-stick cooking spray, making a well in the center. Place empty glass, right side down, in center of dish. Cover with wax paper and cook on high for 18 minutes, rotating 1/4 turn after 6 minutes and again after another 6 minutes of cooking time. Let rest for 5 minutes before serving.

The vegetables add a good flavor to this meat loaf. Use the microwave method and have it ready in less than 30 minutes.

Makes 6 servings

Each Serving

Carb Servings
1

Exchanges
2/3 starch
1 vegetable
3 lean meat

Nutrient Analysis
calories 244
total fat 9g
saturated fat 3mg
cholesterol 71mg
sodium 341mg
total carbohydrate 16g
dietary fiber 2g
sugars 7g
protein 26g

Makes 12 servings

Each Serving

Carb Servings
2

Exchanges
1 1/2 starch
1 vegetable
2 lean meat

Nutrient Analysis
calories 265
total fat 7g
saturated fat 3mg
cholesterol 31mg
sodium 595mg
total carbohydrate 29g
dietary fiber 2g
sugars 7g
protein 21g

Quick Meat Lasagne

1 pound extra lean ground beef or
    ground turkey (7% fat)
1 teaspoon chopped garlic
3/4 teaspoon anise seed
1/2 teaspoon fennel seed
2 cups reduced-fat cottage cheese or
    Ricotta cheese
2 tablespoons dried parsley
4 cups spaghetti sauce (less than 4 g fat
    per 4 ounces)*
3/4 pound uncooked lasagne noodles (12 noodles)
1 cup (4 ounces) grated, reduced-fat
    mozzarella cheese
1/4 cup grated Parmesan cheese

Preheat oven to 350 degrees.

Brown meat and garlic with anise and fennel in a skillet that has sprayed with non-stick cooking spray. Cook until done.

Mix cottage cheese, ground meat and parsley.

Spray a 9-inch by 13-inch baking pan with non-stick cooking spray. Pour 1 cup of sauce in bottom of pan.

Layer in this order: 4 noodles, 1/2 meat mixture, 1/2 mozzarella, 1 cup sauce, 4 noodles, 1/2 meat mixture, 1/2 mozzarella, 1 cup sauce, 4 noodles and the rest of the sauce. Sprinkle with Parmesan cheese.

Bake, covered tightly with aluminum foil, for one hour.

*or one jar (1 pound, 10 ounces) and water to equal 4 cups

Barbecued Smoked Sausage and Cabbage Casserole

4 cups chopped cabbage
1 cup chopped onion
1 cup sliced celery
1 cup sliced bell pepper, red or green
**1 package (16 ounces) low-fat turkey
     smoked sausage, cut into slices**
1/3 cup barbecue sauce

Preheat oven to 350 degrees.

In a large bowl, combine all ingredients and mix well.

Spray a 2 1/2-quart covered casserole with non-stick cooking spray. Add all ingredients.

Cover and bake for 30-40 minutes.

Note: One serving is a good source of fiber.
This recipe is higher in sodium and should be limited by those on a low-sodium diet.

Variation: *Smoked Sausage and Creamy Vegetables* – Substitute 1 can (10 ounces) reduced-fat cream of celery soup for the barbecue sauce. This makes a nice creamy sauce.

Vegetables and smoked sausage go together to make a delicious and healthy dish. The addition of the barbecue sauce adds a good flavor.

Makes 6 cups
5 servings

Each Serving
about 1 cup

Carb Servings
1

Exchanges
1/2 starch
2 vegetable
2 lean meat

Nutrient Analysis
calories 203
total fat 8g
saturated fat 3mg
cholesterol 56mg
sodium 1013mg
total carbohydrate 17g
dietary fiber 3g
sugars 12g
protein 15g

This is another quick-to-prepare casserole that your family will enjoy. We found that stirring halfway through cooking helps to keep the rice moist.

Makes 6 cups
5 servings

Each Serving
about 1 cup

Carb Servings
2

Exchanges
1 2/3 starch
1 vegetable
2 lean meat

Nutrient Analysis
calories 288
total fat 9g
saturated fat 3mg
cholesterol 56mg
sodium 1005mg
total carbohydrate 33g
dietary fiber 3g
sugars 9g
protein 16g

Smoked Sausage and Rice Casserole

1 1/2 cups water
1/3 cup barbecue sauce
1 1/2 cups uncooked quick-cooking brown rice
1 package (16 ounces) low-fat turkey smoked sausage, cut into bite-size pieces
1 cup chopped onion
1 cup sliced celery
1 cup sliced bell pepper, red or green

Preheat oven to 350 degrees.

In a large bowl, mix water and barbecue sauce with rice. Add remaining ingredients and mix well.

Spray a covered 2-quart casserole with non-stick cooking spray. Add all ingredients.

Cover and bake for 45 minutes, stirring halfway through cooking to mix the rice with the liquid.

Stir again before serving.

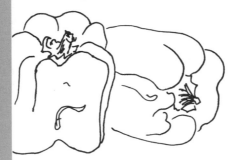

Note: One serving is a good source of fiber. This recipe is higher in sodium and should be limited by those on a low-sodium diet.

Sausage and Sauerkraut

1 jar (32 ounces) sauerkraut
2 cups unpeeled new potatoes, thinly sliced
1/2 cup onion, thinly sliced
**1 pound low-fat turkey smoked sausage, cut
  into 10 pieces**

Drain sauerkraut. Add water and drain. Add water and drain again.

Follow the directions below for microwave or conventional oven.

Conventional Oven: Preheat oven to 350 degrees. Place sauerkraut in a 2-quart covered casserole that has been sprayed with non-stick cooking spray. Top with potatoes, onions and sausage. Cover and cook for 1 hour or until potatoes are tender.

Microwave Oven: Add potatoes and onions to a 2-quart glass covered casserole. Cover and cook on high for 5 minutes, stirring once halfway through cooking time. Top potatoes with sauerkraut and sausage. Cover and microwave on high for 7 minutes, stirring halfway through cooking time.

Note: One serving is an excellent source of fiber. This recipe is higher in sodium and should be limited by those on a low-sodium diet.

Variation: *Sausage and Cabbage* - Substitute shredded cabbage for all or part of the sauerkraut. Cook with potatoes, before adding sausage, when using the microwave.

This quick meal uses low-fat turkey sausage. The sodium from the sauerkraut is significantly reduced by rinsing it twice, however, it can be reduced further by substituting cabbage.

Makes 8 cups
5 servings

Each Serving
about 1 1/2 cups

Carb Servings*
1

Exchanges*
2/3 starch
1 vegetable
2 lean meat

Nutrient Analysis
calories 230
total fat 8g
saturated fat 3mg
cholesterol 56mg
sodium 1272mg
total carbohydrate 22g
dietary fiber 6g
sugars 7g
protein 15g

***reflects carbohydrate
 minus fiber**

This is another complete meal that will be a family pleaser. If you like cabbage more crisp, cook for the lesser amount of time. Ground turkey works best in this recipe.

Makes 8 cups
4 servings

_____

Each Serving
2 cups

Carb Servings*
2

Exchanges*
1 1/2 starch
2 vegetable
3 lean meat

Nutrient Analysis
calories 340
total fat 10g
saturated fat 3mg
cholesterol 67mg
sodium 586mg
total carbohydrate 37g
dietary fiber 5g
sugars 7g
protein 28g

*reflects carbohydrate minus fiber

Creamy Cabbage Stir-fry

4 ounces uncooked egg noodles (eggless) (about 3 cups dry)
1 pound extra lean ground turkey or beef (7% fat)
1 medium onion, chopped, about 1 1/2 cups
1/2 teaspoon salt (optional)
1/4 teaspoon ground black pepper
1 can (10 ounces) reduced-fat cream of celery soup*
4 cups chopped cabbage (about 10 ounces)

Cook noodles according to package directions. Drain.

Spray a large skillet with non-stick cooking spray.

Brown ground meat with onion and seasonings.

Add cream soup and mix well. Add cabbage and reduce heat to low.

Cover and cook for 10-15 minutes or until cabbage is cooked to your liking.

Add cooked noodles and mix well.

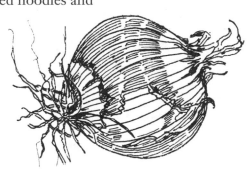

*To reduce sodium, choose soups that are also 30% less sodium.

Note: One serving is an excellent source of fiber.

Bean and Beef/Turkey Enchiladas

1 pound extra lean ground beef or ground turkey (7% fat)
1 cup chopped onion
1 can (31 ounces) fat-free refried beans
1 can (4 ounces) diced green chiles
1/2 teaspoon ground cumin
1/2 teaspoon chili powder
1/2 teaspoon chopped garlic
2 cans (10 ounces each) enchilada sauce
12 tortillas (6-inch) corn or whole wheat, cut into 1-inch strips
1 cup (4 ounces) grated, reduced-fat cheddar cheese or Mexican blend cheese

Preheat oven to 375 degrees. Spray a large skillet with non-stick cooking spray. Add ground meat and onion and cook until done. Remove from heat. Add the next five ingredients and mix well.

Spray a 9-inch by 13-inch baking pan with non-stick cooking spray. Pour 1/2 can of enchilada sauce in the bottom of the pan.

Follow one of the methods below. Bake for 20-25 minutes or until thoroughly heated. Top with cheese and return to oven for 5 minutes.

Layered Method: Layer 1/3 of the tortilla strips, 1/2 of the bean mixture, 1/3 of the tortillas, 1 can sauce, remainder of bean mixture, tortillas and sauce.

Rolled Method: Place filling in each tortilla. Roll to enclose. Place seam side down in baking dish. Pour remaining sauce over top.

Note: One serving is an excellent source of fiber.

Makes 8 servings

Each Serving

Carb Servings*
2

Exchanges*
1 2/3 starch
1 vegetable
2 1/2 lean meat

Nutrient Analysis
calories 330
total fat 9g
saturated fat 3mg
cholesterol 45mg
sodium 1318mg
total carbohydrate 41g
dietary fiber 9g
sugars 2g
protein 23g

***reflects carbohydrate minus fiber**

Makes 12 servings
_____

Each Serving

Carb Servings
2

Exchanges
1 starch
2 vegetable
2 lean meat

Nutrient Analysis
calories 262
total fat 8g
saturated fat 3mg
cholesterol 53mg
sodium 766mg
total carbohydrate 28g
dietary fiber 3g
sugars 6g
protein 20g

Tortilla Pie

2 pounds extra lean ground beef or ground turkey (7% fat)
2 large onions, chopped
2 cups thick and chunky salsa
1 can (8 ounces) tomato sauce*
1 teaspoon each: ground cumin, chili powder and garlic powder
1 can (15 ounces) creamed corn
12 corn tortillas (6-inch), cut into 1-inch strips
1 cup (4 ounces) grated, reduced-fat cheddar cheese or Mexican blend cheese

Preheat oven to 350 degrees.

Spray a large skillet with non-stick cooking spray. Add ground meat and onion and cook until done. Remove from heat.

Add salsa, sauce, seasonings and corn. Mix well.

Spray a 9-inch by 13-inch baking pan with non-stick cooking spray.

Layer mixture with the tortillas, starting with 1/4 of the meat mixture and topping with 1/3 of the tortilla strips. Continue layering, ending with the meat mixture.

Cover and bake for 35-40 minutes or until thoroughly heated.

Add cheese and cook another 5 minutes.

*Sodium is figured for reduced-salt.

Note: One serving is a good source of fiber.

John Torrey

6 ounces uncooked elbow macaroni
1 pound extra lean ground beef or ground
   turkey (7% fat)
1/2 green pepper, chopped
1 small onion, chopped
1 can (14 ounces) diced tomatoes*
1 can (8 ounces) tomato sauce*
1 can (4 ounces) mushroom pieces and
   stems, drained
1/2 cup (2 ounces) cubed, reduced-fat
   cheddar cheese
1/2 teaspoon chopped garlic
1/2 teaspoon chili powder
1/4 teaspoon salt (optional)

Preheat oven to 350 degrees.

Cook macaroni according to package directions. Drain.

Spray a large skillet with non-stick cooking spray. Add ground beef, green pepper and onion. Sauté until meat is cooked.

Add remaining ingredients and macaroni.

Pour into a 2 1/2-quart covered casserole that has been sprayed with non-stick cooking spray.

Bake, covered, for 35-40 minutes or until thoroughly heated.

*Sodium is figured for reduced-salt.

Note: One serving is a good source of fiber.

A friend doubles this recipe when she is entertaining a large group. It can be assembled in advance and refrigerated. Increase cooking time by 15 minutes if it has been refrigerated.

Makes 7 cups
7 servings

Each Serving
1 cup

Carb Servings
2

Exchanges
1 starch
2 vegetable
2 lean meat

Nutrient Analysis
calories 238
total fat 7g
saturated fat 3mg
cholesterol 46mg
sodium 187mg
total carbohydrate 26g
dietary fiber 3g
sugars 6g
protein 19g

Moore

6 ounces uncooked fettucini noodles (eggless)
1 pound extra lean ground beef or ground
   turkey (7% fat)
1 can (10 ounces) tomato soup
1/8 teaspoon ground black pepper
1/4 cup (1 ounce) grated, reduced-fat cheddar
   cheese

Cook fettucini according to package directions. Drain.

Brown meat in a skillet that has been sprayed with non-stick cooking spray. Add soup, pepper and cooked fettucini. Cook over low heat until hot.

Top with cheese and cover for a couple of minutes or until cheese is melted.

Quick Meat and Bean Supper

1 pound extra lean ground beef or ground
   turkey (7% fat)
1/2 cup chopped onion
1 can (15 ounces) fat-free vegetarian baked beans
1/4 cup catsup

Spray a skillet with non-stick cooking spray. Brown ground meat with onion and cook until done.

Add remaining ingredients and heat thoroughly.

Note: One serving is an excellent source of fiber.

Biscuits and Gravy

**1 can (7 ounces) buttermilk biscuits
  (10 biscuits per can)**
1 package (2.6 ounces) low-fat country gravy
**1 pound extra lean ground beef or ground
  turkey (7% fat)**

Prepare the biscuits and country gravy following the package directions.

Meanwhile, cook ground meat in a skillet that has been sprayed with non-stick cooking spray.

When the gravy is thickened, mix with the cooked meat.

To serve, split biscuits and top with gravy.

Note: This recipe is higher in sodium and should be limited by those on a low-sodium diet.

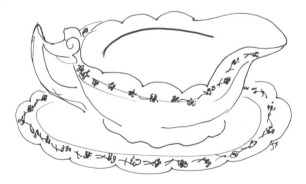

We were able to make a low-fat version of this popular dish. Look for biscuits that are only 100 calories, 1.5 grams of fat and 1 gram fiber for 2 biscuits.

Makes 5 servings

Each Serving

Carb Servings
2

Exchanges
2 starch
2 lean meat
1 fat

Nutrient Analysis
calories 292
total fat 11g
saturated fat 3mg
cholesterol 63mg
sodium 876mg
total carbohydrate 28g
dietary fiber 1g
sugars 6g
protein 22g

Crustless Quiche

1/2 pound extra lean ground beef or ground turkey (7% fat)
1/4 teaspoon salt (optional)
1/8 teaspoon ground black pepper
1 1/2 cups egg substitute (equal to 6 eggs)
1/2 cup nonfat sour cream
1/2 cup nonfat plain yogurt or 1/2 cup nonfat milk
1/3 cup sliced green onion
1/4 cup (1 ounce) grated, reduced-fat cheddar cheese

Preheat oven to 350 degrees.

Brown ground meat, with seasonings, in a skillet that has been sprayed with non-stick cooking spray.

In a medium bowl, using a wire whisk, beat eggs with sour cream and yogurt (or milk) until smooth. Mix in onion and ground meat.

Spray a 9-inch pie pan with non-stick cooking spray.

Pour egg mixture into pan.

Bake for 35 minutes or until a knife inserted in the center comes out clean.

Top with cheese and return to oven for 2 minutes or until cheese is melted.

Desserts

Some of the quick-to-prepare desserts in this section use sugar-free gelatin or sugar-free pudding. Many can be prepared in as little as ten minutes. All of the recipes in this section are lower in sugar and fat than most desserts.

So good and so quick! This impressive dessert can be prepared just a few minutes before company arrives.

Chocolate Mocha Mousse

3 cups nonfat milk
1 tablespoon instant coffee crystals, regular
   or decaffeinated
1 large box (2.1 ounces) sugar-free instant
   chocolate pudding
3 cups nonfat whipped topping
   (8 ounce container)
nonfat whipped topping (optional)

In a medium bowl, mix milk with coffee. Let sit a few minutes then stir until coffee is dissolved.

Add pudding mix and stir constantly with a wire whisk for two minutes.

Refrigerate for 5 minutes.

Add whipped topping and mix well.

Pour into a serving bowl or individual parfait glasses.

Garnish with additional whipped topping, if desired.

This is ready to eat or you can refrigerate it and serve later.

Makes 6 cups
8 servings

Each Serving
3/4 cup

Carb Servings
1

Exchanges
1 1/3 starch

Nutrient Analysis
calories 104
total fat 0g
saturated fat 0mg
cholesterol 2mg
sodium 279mg
total carbohydrate 20g
dietary fiber 1g
sugars 8g
protein 3g

Coffee Mousse

3 cups nonfat milk
2 tablespoons instant coffee crystals, regular or decaffeinated
1 large box (1.5 ounces) sugar-free instant vanilla pudding
3 cups nonfat whipped topping (8 ounce container)
nonfat whipped topping (optional)

In a medium bowl, mix milk with coffee. Let sit a few minutes then stir until coffee is dissolved.

Add pudding mix and stir constantly with a wire whisk for two minutes.

Refrigerate for 5 minutes.

Add whipped topping and mix well.

Pour into a serving bowl or individual parfait glasses.

Garnish with additional whipped topping, if desired.

This is ready to eat or you can refrigerate it and serve later.

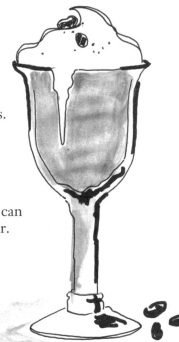

A must for coffee lovers. This light dessert can also be served over angel food cake.

Makes 6 cups
8 servings

Each Serving
3/4 cup

Carb Servings
1

Exchanges
1 starch

Nutrient Analysis
calories 96
total fat 0g
saturated fat 0mg
cholesterol 2mg
sodium 301mg
total carbohydrate 18g
dietary fiber 0g
sugars 8g
protein 3g

This light, refreshing dessert is a good ending to a meal. It can be decorated for the holidays with a miniature candy cane. Sugar-free peppermint candies and candy canes are available.

Makes 4 cups
5 servings

Each Serving
about 3/4 cup

Carb Servings
1

Exchanges
1 starch

Nutrient Analysis
calories 102
total fat 0g
saturated fat 0mg
cholesterol 2mg
sodium 313mg
total carbohydrate 19g
dietary fiber 0g
sugars 8g
protein 3g

Peppermint Mousse

1 small box (1 ounce) sugar-free instant white chocolate pudding
2 cups nonfat milk
1/2 teaspoon peppermint extract
3-4 drops red food coloring
2 cups nonfat whipped topping
5 crushed peppermint candies (optional) regular or sugar-free

In a medium bowl, mix pudding with milk, peppermint extract and food coloring.

Stir constantly with a wire whisk for 2 minutes.

Refrigerate for 5 minutes.

Add whipped topping and mix well.

Spoon into 5 parfait glasses and serve as is or topped with crushed peppermint candies or a candy cane.

White Chocolate Mousse with Berries

1 small box (1 ounce) sugar-free instant white chocolate pudding
2 cups nonfat milk
2 cups nonfat whipped topping
2 cups fresh berries (or frozen, thawed) such as raspberries, blueberries, or huckleberries

In a medium bowl, mix pudding with milk.

Stir constantly with a wire whisk for 2 minutes.

Refrigerate for 5 minutes.

Add whipped topping and mix well.

Layer mousse with berries in a serving bowl or individual parfait glasses. Be sure to save some berries for the top.

This is ready to eat or you can refrigerate it and serve later.

J. STAVER

Try this very light and refreshing dessert. It is so quick to prepare! Use a variety of berries alone or in combination. When fresh berries are not available, substitute frozen berries that have been thawed.

Makes 6 cups
8 servings

Each Serving
3/4 cup

Carb Servings
1

Exchanges
1 starch

Nutrient Analysis
calories 78
total fat 0g
saturated fat 0mg
cholesterol 1mg
sodium 196mg
total carbohydrate 16g
dietary fiber 2g
sugars 6g
protein 2g

This is a refreshing dessert that takes just minutes to prepare. It looks especially good served in individual parfait glasses.

Makes 4 cups
5 servings

Each Serving
about 3/4 cup

Carb Servings
1 1/2

Exchanges
1 1/2 starch

Nutrient Analysis
calories 115
total fat 0g
saturated fat 0mg
cholesterol 2mg
sodium 332mg
total carbohydrate 22g
dietary fiber 0g
sugars 9g
protein 3g

Grasshopper Mousse

1 small box (1 ounce) sugar-free instant white chocolate pudding
2 cups nonfat milk
1/2 teaspoon peppermint extract
3-4 drops green food coloring
2 cups nonfat whipped topping
2 chocolate graham cracker squares, crushed

In a medium bowl, mix pudding with milk, peppermint extract and food coloring.

Stir constantly with a wire whisk for 2 minutes.

Refrigerate for 5 minutes.

Add whipped topping and mix well.

Spoon the pudding mixture in a medium serving bowl or individual parfait glasses.

Top with crushed chocolate graham crackers.

Lemon Parfait

**1 small box (0.3 ounces) sugar-free
   lemon flavored gelatin**
3/4 cup boiling water
1/2 cup very cold water
ice cubes
1 1/2 cups nonfat whipped topping
orange slices for garnish (optional)

Dissolve gelatin in boiling water, stirring constantly for 2 minutes.

Mix 1/2 cup very cold water with ice cubes to make 1 1/4 cups. Add to gelatin, stirring until slightly thickened. Remove any remaining ice cubes.

Add whipped topping and mix well with a wire whisk.

Refrigerate for 30 minutes for a soft set and 1 1/2 hours for a firm set.

Serve in individual parfait glasses or in a large glass bowl. Garnish with orange slices.

Variation: *Layered Parfait* - Double or triple this recipe, using two or three different flavors of gelatin, each prepared separately. Layer each flavor in a large glass serving bowl or parfait glasses. This makes a colorful presentation.

You'll find this creamy dessert to be light and fluffy. The refreshing taste is a great ending to any meal. Any flavor of gelatin can be substituted for the lemon.

Makes 3 1/2 cups
4 servings

Each Serving
3/4 cup

Carb Servings
1/2

Exchanges
2/3 starch

Nutrient Analysis
calories 55
total fat 0g
saturated fat 0mg
cholesterol 0mg
sodium 70mg
total carbohydrate 10g
dietary fiber 0g
sugars 3g
protein 1g

This light dessert tastes and looks so good. It is especially attractive if layered in parfait glasses.

Makes 8 servings

Each Serving

Carb Servings
1 1/2

Exchanges
1 fruit
1 nonfat milk
1 fat

Nutrient Analysis
calories 181
total fat 6g
saturated fat 4mg
cholesterol 23mg
sodium 496mg
total carbohydrate 25g
dietary fiber 1g
sugars 20g
protein 7g

Cream Cheese Dessert

**1 large box (1.5 ounces) sugar-free
   instant vanilla pudding
3 cups nonfat milk
1 tub (12 ounces) light cream cheese
   (room temperature)
1 can (20 ounces) light cherry filling**

In a small mixing bowl, combine pudding mix and milk.

Beat on low speed to mix ingredients.

Add cream cheese. Increase speed and beat until smooth and thickened.

Pour into individual parfait dishes or a large serving dish.

Top with pie filling.

Fruit Pizza For A Crowd

1 package (18 ounces) sugar cookie dough
1 large box (1.5 ounces) sugar-free vanilla
** instant pudding**
3 cups nonfat milk
6 ounces light cream cheese
** (room temperature)**
1 quart strawberries, washed and hulled
** (or other fresh fruit)**

Preheat oven to 350 degrees.

Spray a 16-inch pizza pan with non-stick cooking spray.

Slice cookie dough into 1/4-inch thick slices. Arrange slices on pizza pan so that they are 1/2 to 1-inch apart.

Bake for 18-20 minutes or until golden and set. Cool.

In small mixing bowl, combine pudding mix and milk. Beat on low to mix.

Add cream cheese and beat until smooth and thickened. Pour over cooled cookie crust.

Arrange fruit on top.

Note: This recipe will also make four 8-inch pizzas or one 11-inch by 14-inch *and* an 8-inch pizza. 8-inch cake pans work fine.

I get lots of compliments when I make this because it looks so impressive. The secret is arranging the fruit in an attractive pattern. I often use a combination of strawberries, raspberries, blueberries and kiwi fruit.

Makes 18 servings

Each Serving

Carb Servings
1 1/2

Exchanges
1 starch
1/2 fruit
1 fat

Nutrient Analysis
calories 166
total fat 6g
saturated fat 2mg
cholesterol 55mg
sodium 340mg
total carbohydrate 24g
dietary fiber 1g
sugars 13g
protein 4g

Makes 5 cups
4 servings

Each Serving
1 1/4 cups

Carb Servings
1 1/2

Exchanges
1/2 starch
1 fruit

Nutrient Analysis
calories 100
total fat 0g
saturated fat 0mg
cholesterol 0mg
sodium 58mg
total carbohydrate 22g
dietary fiber 3g
sugars 12g
protein 3g

Strawberries Romanoff

1/2 cup nonfat sour cream
1 tablespoon nonfat milk
1 cup nonfat whipped topping
4 cups sliced strawberries
sugar or artificial sweetener to
**   sweeten strawberries (optional)**
4 whole strawberries for garnish

In a small bowl, mix sour cream with milk.

Using a wire whisk, mix in whipped topping.

Sweeten strawberries, if needed.

Just before serving, layer in individual parfait glasses or in a medium size glass bowl.

Layer in this order: half of the strawberries, half of the sour cream mixture, half of the strawberries, and the remainder of the sour cream mixture.

Garnish with a whole strawberry.

Note: One serving is a good source of fiber.

Variation: *Peaches Romanoff* - substitute fresh peaches for the strawberries.

Cream Cheese Topping

1 small box (1 ounce) sugar-free instant vanilla pudding
2 cups nonfat milk
6 ounces light cream cheese (room temperature)

In a small mixing bowl combine pudding mix and milk. Beat on low speed to mix well.

Add cream cheese. Increase speed and beat until smooth and thick.

Serving tip: Use as a frosting in place of traditional cream cheese frosting. For an attractive dessert, layer with sugar-free flavored gelatin or pudding in parfait glasses.

Makes 2 1/2 cups
20 servings

Each Serving
2 tablespoons

Carb Servings
0

Exchanges
1/3 nonfat milk

Nutrient Analysis
calories 29
total fat 1g
saturated fat 1mg
cholesterol 4mg
sodium 114mg
total carbohydrate 3g
dietary fiber 0g
sugars 2g
protein 2g

Fruit Slush

1/2 - 3/4 cup frozen fruit
1/2 cup nonfat milk, buttermilk or nonfat plain yogurt
1/4 teaspoon vanilla extract
sweetener as needed: about 1-2 teaspoons sugar or the equivalent in artificial sweetener

Blend the first three ingredients until smooth.

Sweeten to taste.

Serving tip: This dessert can be eaten with a spoon or increase the milk and drink it.

Note: One serving is a good source of fiber.

Makes 1 serving

Each Serving

Carb Servings
1

Exchanges
1/2 fruit
1/2 nonfat milk

Nutrient Analysis
calories 91 - with artificial sweetener 74
total fat 0g
saturated fat 0mg
cholesterol 2mg
sodium 51mg
total carbohydrate 17g - with artificial sweetener 13g
dietary fiber 4g
sugars 13g - with artificial sweetener 9g
protein 5g

This old fashioned dessert is good served warm or cold. See page 10 for information on using artificial sweetener.

Makes 8 servings

Each Serving

Carb Servings
1

Exchanges
1/2 starch
2/3 fruit - 1/2 with
   artificial sweetener

Nutrient Analysis
calories 88 - with
   artificial sweetener 68
total fat 1g
saturated fat 0mg
cholesterol 0mg
sodium 16mg
total carbohydrate 19g - with
   artificial sweetener 14g
dietary fiber 2g
sugars 13g - with
   artificial sweetener 8g
protein 1g

Apple Crisp

6 cups peeled, sliced apples
1/4 cup water
2 tablespoons firmly packed brown sugar
   or the equivalent in artificial sweetener
2 teaspoons lemon juice
1 teaspoon ground cinnamon
1/2 cup oats (quick or old fashioned)
1 tablespoon firmly packed brown sugar
   or the equivalent in artificial sweetener
1 tablespoon soft margarine

Preheat oven to 375 degrees.

Combine the first five ingredients and mix well.

Arrange apple mixture in an 8-inch by 8-inch baking dish that has been sprayed with non-stick cooking spray.

Combine remaining ingredients and sprinkle over apples.

Bake for 30 minutes or until apples are tender.

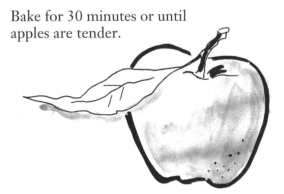

Apple Cake

2/3 cup granulated sugar or the equivalent
   in artificial sweetener
1/2 cup brown sugar
1/2 cup egg substitute (equal to 2 eggs)
1/4 cup vegetable oil (canola)
2/3 cup unbleached all-purpose flour
2/3 cup whole wheat flour
1/2 cup oat bran
1 1/2 teaspoons baking soda
1 teaspoon ground cinnamon
1/4 teaspoon ground allspice
3 cups finely chopped apples (unpeeled)

Optional topping
3/4 cup oats (quick or old fashioned)
1 1/2 tablespoons firmly packed brown sugar
1 1/2 tablespoons soft margarine

Preheat oven to 350 degrees.

In a small bowl mix sugars, egg and oil until well blended.

Mix remaining ingredients, except apples, in a large bowl.

Add egg mixture to dry ingredients and mix just until moistened. Stir in apples.

Pour into a 9-inch by 13-inch baking pan that has been sprayed with non-stick cooking spray.

If using optional topping, combine the ingredients and sprinkle over cake batter.

Bake for 25-30 minutes.

This moist cake is a family favorite. It is a low-sugar and low-fat version of a popular dessert. See page 10 for information on using artificial sweetener.

Makes 16 servings

Each Serving

Carb Servings
1 1/2 - with
   artificial sweetener 1

Exchanges
1 1/2 starch - 1 with
   artificial sweetener
1/2 fat

Nutrient Analysis
calories 142 - with
   artificial sweetener 110
total fat 4g
saturated fat 0mg
cholesterol 0mg
sodium 135mg
total carbohydrate 25g - with
   artificial sweetener 17g
dietary fiber 2g
sugars 15g - with
   artificial sweetener 7g
protein 2g

Makes 12 servings
(plus extra pudding)

Each Serving
1 cup cake

Carb Servings
1 1/2

Exchanges
1 1/2 starch
1/2 fat

Nutrient Analysis
calories 140
total fat 4g
saturated fat 1mg
cholesterol 11mg
sodium 273mg
total carbohydrate 23g
dietary fiber 1g
sugars 3g
protein 3g

Butterfly Cup Cakes

**1 small box (1 ounce) sugar-free instant
  vanilla pudding mix
2 cups nonfat milk
1 dozen cup cakes, yellow or white
2 tablespoons sugar-free preserves
  (raspberry or strawberry)
powdered sugar (optional)**

Make pudding according to package directions, using nonfat milk. Let sit in refrigerator for 5 minutes.

Cut a cone shape from the top of each cup cake, according to diagram, and set aside.

Fill cavity of each cup cake with 1 tablespoon of pudding.

Cut cones in half to make wings.

Place two halves, flat side down, on each cup cake to represent butterfly wings.

Place 1/2 teaspoon of preserves in the center to resemble the body. Dust with powdered sugar (optional).

Variation: *Chocolate Butterfly Cup Cakes* - Substitute chocolate cupcakes and fill with nonfat whipped topping.

Chocolate Cake

3 cups unbleached all-purpose flour
2 cups granulated sugar
1/2 cup unsweetened cocoa powder
2 teaspoons baking soda
1 teaspoon salt (optional)
2 cups cold water
2/3 cup oil (canola)
2 tablespoons vinegar
2 teaspoons vanilla extract

Preheat oven to 350 degrees.

Mix the first five ingredients in a large bowl.

Mix the remaining ingredients in a small bowl. Add
to dry ingredients and mix until smooth.

Pour into a 9-inch by 13-inch baking pan that has been
sprayed with non-stick cooking spray.

Bake for 35-40 minutes.

Variations: *Chocolate Cupcakes* - Pour batter into 24 cupcake tins
that have been sprayed with non-stick cooking spray. Bake for
20-25 minutes.
Smaller cake (8-inch by 8-inch) - Halve all of the ingredients and
bake for 25 minutes.

*Chocolate lovers will
really enjoy this moist
cake. Serve plain or
top with nonfat
whipped topping. See
page 10 for information
on using artificial
sweetener.*

Makes 16 servings

Each Serving

Carb Servings
3

Exchanges
3 starch
1 fat

Nutrient Analysis
calories 273
total fat 10g
saturated fat 1 mg
cholesterol 0mg
sodium 158mg
total carbohydrate 45g
dietary fiber 2g
sugars 25g
protein 0g

Makes 9 servings

Each Serving

Carb Servings
1 1/2 - with
    artificial sweetener 1

Exchanges
1 1/2 starch - 1 1/3 with
    artificial sweetener

Nutrient Analysis
calories 134 - with
    artificial sweetener 112
total fat 3g
saturated fat 0mg
cholesterol 0mg
sodium 154mg
total carbohydrate 24g - with
    artificial sweetener 18g
dietary fiber 1g
sugars 13g - with
    artificial sweetener 8g
protein 2g

Mandarin Orange Cake

1 cup unbleached all-purpose flour
1/2 cup granulated sugar OR 1/4 cup of sugar
    ***and* the equivalent in artificial sweetener**
    for 1/4 cup sugar
1 teaspoon baking soda
1/2 teaspoon salt (optional)
1 can (11 ounces) mandarin oranges, drained
1/4 cup egg substitute (equal to 1 egg)
2 tablespoons oil (canola)
1 teaspoon vanilla extract

Preheat oven to 350 degrees.

Mix the first four ingredients in a medium bowl.

Combine the remaining ingredients, mashing the oranges. Combine with the dry ingredients and mix well.

Pour into an 8-inch by 8-inch baking pan that has been sprayed with non-stick cooking spray.

Bake for 30-35 minutes.

Pineapple Cake

2 cups unbleached all-purpose flour
1 cup granulated sugar OR 1/2 cup sugar
   ***and* the equivalent in artificial sweetener**
   for 1/2 cup sugar
2 teaspoons baking soda
1/4 teaspoon salt (optional)
1 can (20 ounces) unsweetened crushed
   pineapple, in juice (not drained)
1/2 cup egg substitute (equal to 2 eggs)

Preheat oven to 350 degrees.

Combine the first four ingredients in a medium bowl.

Mix pineapple with egg substitute. Add to dry ingredients and mix until blended.

Pour into a 9-inch by 13-inch baking pan that has been sprayed with non-stick cooking spray.

Bake for 30-35 minutes.

This moist cake does not use any fat. It can be served plain, or with nonfat whipped topping. Cream Cheese Topping (page 245) is also good on this cake. See page 10 for information on using artificial sweetener.

Makes 16 servings

Each Serving

Carb Servings
2 - with
   artificial sweetener 1 1/2

Exchanges
1 1/4 starch - 1 with
   artificial sweetener
1/2 fruit

Nutrient Analysi s
calories 121 - with
   artificial sweetener 96
total fat 0g
saturated fat 0mg
cholesterol 0mg
sodium 172mg
total carbohydrate 28g - with
   artificial sweetener 21g
dietary fiber 1g
sugars 15g - with
   artificial sweetener 9g
protein 3g

indicates variation

indicates variation

indicates variation

indicates variation

* *indicates variation*

indicates variation

indicates variation

indicates variation

* *indicates variation*

Order Form

Products from ScaleDown Publishing, Inc., by Brenda J. Ponichtera, R.D.

- **Quick & Healthy Low-fat, Carb Conscious Cooking**
- **Quick & Healthy Volume II**
- **Reproducible Masters**

Telephone orders: 541-296-5859. Please have your Visa or MasterCard ready.
Fax orders: 541-296-1875
Postal orders: ScaleDown Publishing, 1519 Hermits Way, The Dalles, Oregon 97058
E-mail: scaledwn@gorge.net • http://www.quickandhealthy.net
**Call for quantity (6 or more) discount - for resale only.

Books

Quick & Healthy Low-fat, Carb Conscious Cooking, $18.95 .... $ _____
Quick & Healthy Volume II, $16.95 .... $ _____

Reproducible Masters

Menus & Recipes Set 1 (English), $65.00 .... $ _____
Menus & Recipes Set 1 (Spanish), $65.00 .... $ _____
Menus & Recipes Set 2 (English), $65.00 .... $ _____
Menus & Recipes Set 2 (Spanish), $65.00 .... $ _____
Ideas for Meals without recipes (English), $25.00 .... $ _____
Ideas for Meals without recipes (Spanish), $25.00 .... $ _____
Weight Loss/Low-Fat (English), $30.00 .... $ _____
Weight Loss/Low-Fat (Spanish), $30.00 .... $ _____
Eating Out & Holidays (English only), $30.00 .... $ _____

Shipping

$3.50 for first book, $2.00 for each additional book .... $ _____
$4.00 per reproducible masters packet .... $ _____

Total Enclosed .... $ _____

Payment   ☐ Check   ☐ Visa   ☐ MasterCard

Card Number_____ Expiration Date _____ /_____

Name on Card _____ Signature _____

Ship to

Name _____

Address _____ City/State/Zip _____

Telephone _____ E-mail _____

ENJOY LOW-FAT, CARB CONSCIOUS MEALS

All those who just want to eat better - as well as anyone with heart disease, diabetes or who want to lose weight - will welcome this long-awaited 2nd edition of the award-winning, Quick & Healthy Recipes and Ideas — over 500,000 sold!

Of the more than 200 delicious quick-to-prepare recipes, over 60 are new and the rest have been updated for current times. The sensible use of carbs features whole grains and high fiber foods while limiting simple carbs.

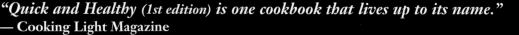

Special features to help you save time & stay healthy

Over 200 low-fat, carb conscious recipes
- over 90 with 0-10 grams of carb per serving
- over 90 with 11-25 grams of carb per serving
- over 30 with 26-35 grams of carb per serving

Detailed nutritional analysis for each recipe, including
- food exchanges for weight loss and diabetes
- fiber, carb servings, fat, and more

Easy to follow low-fat menus

Tips for trimming fat and sodium from your diet

A listing of foods and their fiber content

Conventional and microwave directions

Time Saving Ideas, Weight Loss & Exercise Tips, and Products Worth Trying

"Quick and Healthy (1st edition) is one cookbook that lives up to its name."
— Cooking Light Magazine

Brenda J. Ponichtera is a registered dietitian, speaker and author. Her busy private practice in Oregon, specializing in diabetes, weight loss and heart disease—and her books— have positively effected the lives of many. As a medical professional and teacher, Brenda has focused on helping people develop healthful, lifelong eating habits. Brenda lives in The Dalles, Oregon with her husband and two cats.

ISBN 0-9629160-2-1

51895>

9 780962 916021

$18.95